Whoops, there it goes again!

How to stay positive when the bottom keeps dropping out of your world.

by

Jo Richings

DEDICATION

This book is dedicated to my Mum.

They say that hearts don't break, God, But that's not always true.
The day you took our Mum away,
You broke our hearts in two.
Look around your garden Lord,
She won't be hard to find,
She has a face that's full of love
And a heart that's good and kind.
Tell that we love her
And when you see her smile,
Put your arms around her
And hold her for a while!

I miss you so much Mum xxx.

CONTENTS

ACKNOWLEDGEMENTS

Massive gratitude to the wonderful friends and family who have supported me through some pretty challenging times.

In particular:

My amazing kids, Abby & Sam

I couldn't be prouder of you both. The strength you both showed through some very difficult times has been just astounding.

My fabulous family

My Dad, my wonderful sister Aly and her lovely family.

My lovely friends

In particular Caroline, Cath, Rob, Bev, Natalie, Michelle, Nicki, Jackie, Amanda, Peter, Sue, Marie, Simon and Helga.

I love you all bucketfuls.

My wonderful readers and editor

Thank you to the lovely people that gave up their time to read and edit this book, especially Kate Jones but also massive gratitude to Sarah Clark, Michelle Hazelwood and Catherine Gray.

Introduction

Hello and welcome! It's lovely to have you here.

Let's jump straight in with a couple of questions...

Do any of the following sound familiar?

- Do you feel like life keeps on throwing you curveballs? Curveballs like divorce, redundancy, bereavement or illnesses?
- Are you are struggling to stay positive—or worse, are you depressed?
- Do you put on your "happy face" to the world, but inside are you desperately unhappy?
- Do you want to change, know you must change, but don't know how?
- Do you wish life could be better, that you could be happier?
- Do you start projects—perhaps a diet or exercise regime—only to quit within a month (or a week)?
- Do you lack self-confidence or self-belief?
- Do you feel rubbish about yourself most of the time?
- Does your inner critic chatter endlessly, telling you how bad you are, how fat you are, how ugly you are, or how stupid you are?
- Are you an incredible procrastinator? Has "I'll start again on Monday" become your mantra?
- Do you have difficult health, relationship, or career challenges that are getting you down?

According to Jim Butcher:

"The human mind isn't a terribly logical or consistent place. Most people, given a choice to face a hideous or terrifying truth or to conveniently avoid it, choose the convenience and peace of normality. That doesn't make them strong or weak people, or good or bad people. It just makes them people."

Hmmm... good point, Jim! It's so much easier not to deal with our "stuff"—to stick our heads in the sand and pretend that everything is fine. Easier, maybe, but it certainly doesn't make us happier.

So... this book is for people who want to:

- Be happier.
- Worry less.
- Stop procrastinating.
- Feel good about themselves.
- Improve their relationships.
- Be more positive and motivated.
- Create some new, positive, and powerful habits.
- Increase their self-esteem and self-confidence.
- Have the courage to step out of their comfort zone.
- Develop their emotional resilience muscle, so they are better equipped to cope with the curveballs.

If any of the above resonates with you, then great, you're in the right place! I believe reading this book will increase your chances of success tenfold.

Part One of *Whoops, There It Goes Again* is a whistle-stop tour of my story. It's a story of domestic violence, failed marriages, debt, obesity, cheating husbands, breast cancer and losing my Mum. And these are just some the things that have caused the bottom to drop out of my world. But it's also a story of hope. I've learned that when life throws you a curveball, rather than sitting around and throwing a pity party, you just have to knock the damn thing the hell out of the park! I write from the heart – no holds barred. My story is intended to make you laugh, inspire you to look at what's not working in your own life and to remind you that hard times don't mean the game is over.

I've learned that the only thing we can expect in life is for things to happen as they will, outside of our control or our plans. In some cases, that just happens to be the bottom dropping out of our world—at least one, twice, or sometimes more. Some of you, like me, will have only just started the "repair job" when it will drop out from under you again.

That's life, I'm afraid. Curveballs are to be expected. Awful illnesses, life-threatening diseases, heart-breaking losses, messy breakups and soul-destroying divorces, wayward kids, mounting debts, bankruptcy, hating your job or losing your job, and losing your business are all part of life's rich tapestry. I passionately believe that armed with the simple tools and strategies you will learn in Part Two of this book; you will be able to build your emotional resilience muscle to overcome ANY challenge, now and in the future. When things are tough, remind yourself that your track record for getting through bad days so far is 100%, and that's pretty good. Your body and heart will heal, new relationships will blossom, kids will get back on track, and new jobs or careers will appear on the horizon. That's what makes life so exciting, we never quite know what is around the corner.

The first part of this book is my story so far, and the second includes all the tips, tools, tricks, and techniques I've used over the last 27 years since I picked up my very first book on personal development at the age of 21. That book was *The Power of Your Subconscious Mind* by Joseph Murphy, and what I learned changed my life in so many marvellous and wondrous ways.

Reading *The Power of Your Subconscious Mind* created a hunger for knowledge that has never been satiated. Since then, I have read hundreds of books, listened to thousands of hours of audio-books, watched countless hours of videos and DVDs, and attended many seminars, conferences, and retreats. Personal development became my work, my hobby, and my life. Over the last 27 years, I have extensively studied positive psychology, cognitive behavioural therapy, neuro-linguistic programming, the biology of beliefs, the power of habits, mindfulness, meditation and neuroplasticity.

During my nine years as a Licenced Certified Coach with ActionCoach, the largest coaching franchise in the world, I worked with hundreds of clients, helping them not only to create successful businesses but also to create happier and more fulfilling lives for themselves and their families. I have worked with the most wonderful people, from business owners, chief execs and managing directors to 18-year-old students, grandmothers and homemakers.

After discovering EFT (Emotional Freedom Technique), the most exciting tool I have learned in 27 years, I studied to become a practitioner and qualified in 2014. I love learning about why we do what we do (or why we don't do what we know we should do!), and with every book or audio comes a new level of understanding.

How to get the best out of Part Two.

Part Two is designed to be read like a manual. But much more fun, interesting and life-changing!

It's a book that you can dip in and out of, or read as it is laid out for you. It's entirely up to you. You will find a huge amount of information in Part Two, some will be relevant to you right now and some won't. Don't feel that you have to incorporate *everything* into your life straight away.

As this is my first book, I am excited to share all my knowledge with you. I want you to have the same tools at your disposal that I had when I went through some very challenging times. But I am also very conscious that I don't want you to get so overwhelmed with lots of new concepts and practices that you get even more stressed than you currently may be. Just choose one or two things at a time. Apply them. Play with them. Get used to them and practise them until you notice that not only are they helping you to feel better, but they are starting to become a habit.

I have created templates to help you with the exercises which you can download at www.jorichings.com/whoops, and I have also included a downloadable "mind map" to help you remember what you are learning.

Mind maps are a brilliant tool to help you to internalise and understand what you are reading. Have you ever read, listened or watched something that you thought was interesting and useful, only to completely forget about it within a few weeks?

According to Atkinson and Schiffrin, this is because new information is stored in your short-term memory, which if recalled, will move to your long-term memory. Apparently, we can only hold approximately seven pieces of new information at any one time so if you don't use it – you lose it. Glancing at the mind map regularly and recalling what you have learned so far will help move this information to your long-term memory – meaning you are much most likely to remember it and act on it.

Print the mind map and keep it in the front of this book while you are reading (or near your Kindle) and each time you pick up the book to read, quickly recap the mind map sections you have already read. This simple exercise will do more for ensuring that this book makes a difference to your life than anything else.

At the end of each chapter, I have also included "Chapter in a nutshell" and "Action from the chapter" sections to help you recall what you are learning.

Life According to Jo

Like many people who have dedicated their lives to being the best they can be, I have been inspired by countless amazing mentors. Each gifted me with a golden nugget or two, which I've thrown into the "mix" to create my unique philosophy on life. People like Zig Ziglar, Tony Robbins, Jim Rohn, Brenden Burchard, Oprah, Napoleon Hill, Joseph Murphy, Marissa Peer, Mel Roberts, Jack Canfield, Marci Shimoff, Wayne Dyer, Louise Hay, Charles Duhigg, Anita Moorjani, Mike Dooley, Carol Dweck, Dr Steve Peters, Ester Hicks, Eckhart Toile, Deepak Chopra, Gregg Braden, Brice Lipton, Stephen Covey, Rhonda Bryne, Joe Vitale, Tim Ferris and Brian Tracy (just to name a few) have all enriched my life with their teachings, and for that, I am massively grateful. I have taken what resonated with me from each book or audio, and the result is "Life According to Jo"—the philosophy you will read in this book.

This is one thing I encourage each of you to do. I encourage you to create your unique philosophy by trying this stuff out, seeing how it works for you. Take on the bits you like and leave the rest. Then read another book and do the same. And another. And another. You'll find that we all approach personal change through a different lens, each bringing a new perspective to the fundamental underlying truths. As you read each book, your level of belief and understanding will grow deeper and deeper.

In Part Two, you will learn the exact techniques that have enabled me to:

- Stay positive and motivated despite numerous curveballs.
- Transform from an unhappy, stressed, obese workaholic who never exercised, to a happy, relaxed, fit, and one-hundred-pounds-lighter lover of life.
- Build a prosperous and abundant career doing the things that make my heart sing such as writing, speaking, and coaching.
- Become a successful social entrepreneur creating tools, programmes, and apps that make a positive difference in the world, including HappiMe—an innovative app aimed at raising self-esteem and happiness levels in children, young people, and adults.
- Create a level of wealth, happiness, and abundance in my life that I'm immensely grateful for every day.

"I have read many inspirational books, but Jo's positive, infectious, and straight-forward approach beats all of them. I have never been so moved, inspired, and determined to overcome and change.

Jo's story is emotional, but she explains how she turned her life around. It's extraordinary. She clearly outlines the steps she took to conquer some traumatic experiences and why she now teaches these techniques to help others. I learned so much. I now have a 'toolbox' of strategies, tips, and techniques to raise my game and take on and succeed at anything I put my mind to. Everyone should read this wonderful book."–Michelle,

What You Will Learn in This Book:

- Why we do what we do (or don't do what we should do).
- Why we procrastinate, and most importantly, how to stop!
- Goal-setting—why traditional goal-setting methods don't work.
- Why success from "thinking positively" is all a big lie.
- How to manage your inner critic and empower your inner coach.
- How to create new positive, empowering beliefs—the only way to ensure long-term changes in your life.
- How to activate the Law of Attraction to create wealth and abundance in your life.
- The tools, strategies, tips and ideas to help you improve any area of your life.
- How to keep a positive attitude and stay on track, even when all hell is breaking loose around you.
- The self-motivation, drive and passion to be the best you can be!

"An inspirational and motivational story, delivered with humour, vulnerability, deep understanding, and warmth. I can't think of anyone who would not benefit from reading this book. Thank you, Jo."

–Rob Carter, Business Coach

This book is written as though I'm talking to a good friend or a favourite client. I'm going to talk to you about some stuff I never told anyone until just recently. I want to create a space where you are ready to be truly honest with yourself and to do that; I believe I need to bare my soul too. I want you to read my story and think, "wow, if Jo can go through all that and remain reasonably positive, then so can I". Because you can. Some of you may even be going through similar, or worse things right now. If so, I hope you can take courage from my story.

Imagine that I'm a close friend committed to helping you become the best you can be. The best parent, employee, business owner, daughter, friend—the best human being. Think of me as your coach. Or an older, slightly bossy (but very wise) sister. You'll notice I'm a bit of a "say it as it is, no nonsense" kind of girl. Please take my advice in the spirit in which it is given—with much love, empathy for whatever your current situation is, and endless amounts of encouragement. I'm your cheerleader, your coach, your sensible (and wise, did I mention wise?) friend. I passionately believe there is greatness in you and that you can have whatever you want in life if you're prepared to follow some simple steps with consistency.

The fact that you have picked up this book tells me some very important things about you. First up... you have good taste! But seriously. You're ready for change. You're fed up with being fed up and are prepared to get off your backside and do something about it once and for all. Finally, you're part of the top 1-3% of people in the world who have read a personal development book! That's a great start.

I think it's terribly sad that millions and millions of people around the word live unhappy, unfulfilled lives. They're in jobs they hate, relationships that aren't right for them, and bodies they're not happy with, living lives without passion or purpose. If any of those things resonate with you, you've picked up the right book. This book will work if you do the work.

If you're a personal development junkie and have

bookshelves full of motivational books you've never acted on, let's get one thing straight right now. This is a WORKBOOK— which means you have to get off your butt and actually do the mindset exercises in Part Two, especially the 30-Day Challenge. No excuses.

If you were once an "I'll read the book first and then come back to the exercises later" kind of person, you no longer are that person. Okay? You are now a doer. A person of action. Make that your first commitment to yourself.

Being brutally honest, if you're not going to do the exercises, you'd just as well pop this book into the local charity shop so someone who really wants to change can read it. Don't be that person. Please. Because I believe you can have the life of your dreams. You just have to take the first steps.

In Part One, I have shared my story to give you some context to Part Two, and so you will understand what I have been through. That said, if you are not interested in reading my story, please feel free to jump straight into Part Two. I absolutely won't be offended. Look at this almost as two separate books. I hope this book will bring you inspiration, motivation, strategies for success, happiness, and abundance.

I'm looking forward to helping you make the changes you need to live the life of your dreams. The life you deserve.

With much love

Jo

xxx

PART ONE: MY JOURNEY

"When we stop judging ourselves, we start loving ourselves."

Jo Richings

The First Nine Years

The first eight or nine years of my life were pretty normal. I was the youngest of two girls and definitely the boisterous one. My poor Mum didn't know what hit her when I came along after three years of caring for my much quieter sibling. My lovely sister Aly and I are like chalk and cheese.

We lived in a three-bedroom semi in a nice, quiet part of Bristol. Mum worked weekends as a cook at our local hospital, and Dad was a self-employed electrician. He was a tad grumpy most of the time, but other than that, my childhood was ordinary.

Dad was quite strict compared to many of my friends' parents; this caused argument after argument as I grew up. I couldn't see the sense of making us come home an hour earlier than everyone else, especially when that meant we had to walk home alone because everyone else stayed out later.

Catching pneumonia the day after I was born had resulted in some nasty chest problems throughout my childhood. I was at the doctor's regularly with infection after infection, so much so that Mum used to keep antibiotics in the house for me. Life got a little rough sometimes, as I developed asthma, constantly puffing on inhalers. I seemed to be allergic to

17

everything from dust to animal fur, so I spent most of my time coughing, especially at night.

Mum and Dad tried everything to stop these coughing attacks, from tilting my bed to installing smelly lamps that were kept burning throughout the night. They boiled the kettle in my room through the night to produce steam in my bedroom. Every morning, I put my head over a bowl of steaming menthol with a towel over my head to keep in the steam. This was always followed by "tipping", which I hated. I had to lie over a low stool with my head near the ground while some well-meaning adult pummelled the hell out of my back to loosen the catarrh! It was gross, and it hurt.

The coughing was so bad that my parents took turns sleeping downstairs so at least one of them could get a good night's sleep. Bless them...

Most of the families moved onto our street at the same time, and all had kids of similar ages. We played "knock out ginger" (much to the annoyance of the neighbours), "pick up sticks" on the roundabout in the park and "hide-and-seek" in the streets.

Every summer, five or six families on the street would go away on holiday together to holiday camps around the Devon and Cornwall coast. We would all set off in a big convoy to create some of the best memories of my childhood.

WHOOPS ROUND 1: CHILD ABUSE

*"You have to have the bad days to appreciate the good ones." –
Unknown*

One of these family holidays changed everything for me. We
were pretty much left to our own devices for most of the day
and evening, just returning to our parents for food or change
for the arcade. Looking back on it now, I guess we were easy
prey for anyone who thought to take advantage of us.

I was "befriended" by a man who worked as part of the
entertainment team at the holiday camp. I won't go into
detail, but let's just say he had no right being around
children. What happened to me wasn't as horrendous as
what many people have endured, but it was enough to leave a
huge impact on the next 35 years of my life.

Already a chubby kid, I turned to food for comfort and buried
the shame of what had happened in layers of fat. I also buried
the memories. I locked them away in a closed box and didn't
open that box again until I was 25 years old. I have since
discovered that comfort-eating and blocking out the
memories are really common coping mechanisms in people
who have suffered child abuse.

It seems that every time I turn on the TV or radio nowadays,
there's yet another horrific child abuse scandal dating back to
a similar time. It was far more common than anyone realised.

I understand a lot more about child abuse now. I understand
that paedophiles seem to be able to sense when a child has
been damaged, and four years later, it happened again—this

time with a local man.

My Relationship with Food

"If food is your best friend, it's also your worst enemy." – Edward "Grandpa" Jones

Let's face it... snacks like crisps, chocolate, and fatty foods taste good. They are designed to taste good. Most people, including myself, learn to associate food with feeling loved, feeling good, and being cared for. We use food as a reward, something to make us feel better after a bad day. Sweets after school, pudding if we eat our main meal, cake on birthdays, takeaways as treats, a glass of wine after a hard day—they all help us come to the following conclusion:

If we are feeling good, bad or indifferent, yay—food is the answer.

So, we eat, and initially, we may feel better, particularly because we typically choose "comfort foods"—high-fat, high-starch, or high-sugar foods like ice cream, pizza, or chocolate. These foods also spike certain neurotransmitters in the brain, which is why we initially feel so good. And then we crash. We feel even more depressed, ashamed, and disappointed. And then, guess what? We eat to feel better! Or we go on a mad diet; determined things will be different. We fail. We eat. And around and around the vicious cycle goes. This is what happened to me. Not only was I overeating because it tasted good – I was also eating because I was lonely and ashamed.

Food became my friend. I would stop in the shops on the way home from school, buy sweets and chocolate, and hide them in my room. I would sneak into the kitchen and raid the biscuit tin as often as I could get away with it. Overeating simply became a habit, a "programme" I was running.

At 10, I weighed 10 stone (140 pounds), and by the time I was 16, I weighed 16 stone (224 pounds). I was bullied relentlessly about my weight for years. Not only was I overweight, I also wore glasses (white NHS glasses... Really, Mum? What were you thinking?) and my surname was Smith. I might just as well have had "victim" tattooed on my forehead.

WHOOPS ROUND 2: THE BULLYING

"Courage doesn't always roar. Sometimes courage is the quiet voice at the end of the day saying, 'I will try again tomorrow'."
–Mary Anne Radmacher

It didn't take me long to understand that kids can be cruel. They can be spiteful, vindictive, and downright horrible. I remember the first time I was bullied. It filled me with this awful despair that I wasn't good enough. If I were good enough, people would be nicer to me, surely? They wouldn't call me names like "fatty," "fatso," and "four eyes". They wouldn't sneer and ask, "who ate all the Smiths crisps?" (a popular brand back then). I can remember feeling a sense of bewilderment. Why would they do that? I wouldn't dream of saying horrible things to someone to make them feel bad.

One older boy who lived behind our house made my life a misery for months as he followed me home from school, shouting abusive names and pushing me about. After one particularly bad day when he hit me, I finally plucked up the courage to tell my Dad he was picking on me. I was met with the advice, "clout him back. He'll leave you alone then".

The next day, he happened to be in my garden, picking on me at the same time as I had a heavy broom in my hand. In my defence, I did warn him that if he didn't leave me alone, I was going to whack him around the head with the broom. He thought I was joking... I wasn't. The broom connected with the side of his head quite nicely! Thanks, Dad. Looking back, I'm not sure this was the best parenting advice in the world, but it did the trick. He left me alone, unfortunately to be replaced by numerous others.

Over the years, I became quite adept at fighting my corner and built up a bit of a reputation as someone you didn't want to mess with. I had created a big "front" that stayed with me for years. Like many overweight kids, I understood that if you laughed with the bullies, they gave up quite quickly, so I worked hard to get them on my side. I created this "Happy Jo" persona—on the outside, I was bubbly and happy, but on the inside, I felt sad, helpless, and broken. I had well and truly blocked out the memories of the child abuse at this point, so I could never quite work out why I was so unhappy. I just blamed it on my weight. I tried to lose weight over and over but always ended up back where I started—or heavier (which makes you feel even worse about yourself, as I'm sure some of you will understand from personal experience). This was the start of years of yo-yoing between dieting and bingeing. I couldn't find a happy medium.

Every time I lost weight and gained it again, I seemed to lose a little part of myself—a little bit more self-respect. I felt this awful despair. Being overweight and unhappy with your body impacts everything about your life. Getting invited out would send me into a spin, worrying about what to wear, and planning a holiday in a hot country would send me into a meltdown over what I would look like on the beach or if I would even fit into the plane seat. These anxieties grew so overwhelming that I avoided holidays for years as I got older.

I want to add here that I'm not saying every overweight person had a horrible childhood, as that is not the case. Long-term overeating can start much later in life and is not always tied to bad experiences or even your emotions. Overeating can just become a bad habit. High-fat and high-sugar foods taste good, eating it makes us feel good, and it's natural to want to do more of what feels good.

Drink and Drugs

"Bad habits are like chains that are too light to feel until they are too heavy to carry." –Warren Buffet

For as long as I can remember, I felt I was different to other people. I felt numb inside, almost like I was in a bubble watching everyone from afar. Everyone else seemed happy and confident. Nobody else seemed to hate themselves as I did. I started to drink quite heavily, and for a while, I got in with a really bad crowd. We experimented with the drug of the day—glue sniffing. Getting high or drunk helped me block out my life, allowing me to stop thinking about my problems or my weight.

WHOOPS ROUND 3: BEING A PUNCHING BAG

"Don't let what others think decide who you are." –Dennis Rodman

Unfortunately, my low self-worth led me to the kind of men who would take advantage of me, and between the ages of 16 and 21, I was in two relationships with men who used me as a punching bag. One hit me just for the fun of it and the other whenever he had been drinking. I thought it was my fault. That I deserved it. I wasn't worth a nicer man. I carried on eating to smother my feelings of despair, hurt, and shame. I had developed a habit of overeating, bingeing and dieting that stayed with me for the next 23 years.

I now understand that when your energy is low, you attract other people and situations at the same energy level, and they're likely to take advantage of you. Like definitely attracts like. More on that later.

The first time someone hit me, I was 16 years old and in a "relationship" with a guy named Jim, who was ten years older than me. I had met him on the CB radio, which was our version of WhatsApp, I guess. You would chat to someone over the radio and arrange to meet them, which, looking back, was pretty dangerous. It didn't seem dangerous at the time though. I met the man I later married on the CB, and my lovely sister Aly is still married to her first love—a guy she also met through the CB.

At first, I was flattered, as he was much older than me. But I soon came to realise that he was a bit of a psychopath. He rapidly became possessive and controlling, and within weeks, I felt like I couldn't get away. He told me multiple times that he would never let me leave him, and that if he couldn't have me, no one could—he'd just kill me. He was a frightening, awful man on so many levels, but I had no idea how to get away from him. One day, he didn't like what I said, so he just started punching me. And I mean really punching me. I realised that those stars you see on cartoons are actually real—I saw stars myself.

I would like to say that this was the wake-up call I needed, but it wasn't. I kidded myself that I liked being with him—he was exciting and dangerous—but in reality, I felt scared and stuck and couldn't see a way out.

My parents threw a fit when they met him; they could see right away what a horrendous guy he was. He was cocky and full of himself—definitely not the kind of man they wanted to see their daughter dating.

After we were together for a few months, my parents, my sister, and I went on a camping holiday to Tenby in West Wales. I was under strict instructions to call him at a certain time each day, and because I missed calling him one day, he just turned up at the campsite—totally out of the blue and without even a change of clothes. When I heard him shout my name across the car park, my blood ran cold. He had decided to hitchhike the 130 miles to "see me", bordering on the line between a boyfriend and a stalker.

Sensing how dangerous he was, my parents tried to ban me from seeing him. Their decree went along the lines of, "If you live in this house, you live by these rules". That was all a rebellious 17-year-old needed to hear. I moved out and into a shared flat with Jim in a rough part of town. We lived with a sweet old alcoholic called Kenny, who turned out to be my saviour. At first, he kept to himself, obviously picking up on how dangerous Jim was. He didn't want to get involved, but after some time, we started talking when Jim was out.

By this time, Jim was hitting me pretty much on a daily basis if he didn't like what I was said or wore, or sometimes he'd hit me just because he wanted to pick a fight. Kenny could hear what was going on through the thin walls and kept telling me I needed to leave Jim.

One morning after a particularly bad night, Kenny stepped into the living room with tears in his eyes and told me I had to leave that day. He helped me pack up my things and took me to the telephone box to call my Dad. I swallowed my pride and called my parents, asking them to get me. We had hardly spoken since I'd moved out—Dad refused to let me speak to Mum because I was "breaking her heart"—so I wasn't sure what reaction I would get. But they welcomed me back with open arms.

Life was pretty difficult for a while after that. Jim still followed me around, hanging out in front of the house and my work. We called the police on numerous occasions, and I heard much later that he had beaten Kenny and smashed up the man's flat, which made me so sad. I often wonder if Kenny's still alive. I hope so.

Eventually, things calmed down, and I thought Jim had moved on. Then, one day as I was driving to work on my little moped, he jumped out into the middle of the road right in front of me. He wanted to show me his new tattoo— "Jo Forever". He'd totally lost touch with reality. I rode off quickly, telling him I was late for work and called the police again as soon as I got there. The police came and took a statement and asked if I wanted to press charges as they had told him numerous times to stay away from me. I decided not to – I just wanted him out of my life. Thank goodness that was the end of it all and I never saw him again.

A few months later, I met Mike. Mike was completely different to Jim—he was good-looking, kind, gentle, funny, and we got on brilliantly. We met through mutual friends on the CB radio, and it was love at first sight for both of us. He was a couple of years older than me and had a steady job as a service engineer. My parents loved him, and I had a great relationship with his family. We were great together. One of my favourite times was when we saved up to go away on holiday. We stayed in a grotty little caravan in Devon. We didn't have much money, it rained pretty much every day and the cupboard where the vacuum was stored smelt as if something had died in it, but we still had the most wonderful time. He knew what had happened with Jim and was so loving and gentle with me. I was ridiculously happy! Life was good.

After we'd been together for about 18 months, he was offered a promotion, which involved a transfer to Swansea. House prices were rising dramatically in Bristol and were much cheaper in Wales, so when I was 19, we decided to move to Swansea. We rented for six months, then found a lovely little house on a road I couldn't pronounce.

Things were brilliant for a while, life was exciting, and I enjoyed playing "house", then after a while, the pressure of being away from our friends and families started to have an impact.

WHOOPS ROUND 4: BETRAYAL

"Stand up to your obstacles and do something about them. You will find that they haven't half the strength you think they have." –Norman Vincent Peale

Mike grew lazy and would finish work a few hours earlier than I. I'd found a good job as a cook in a nursing home, but the hours were really long – I left home at 5.30am and got home at 6.30pm each day. When I came home from work, I'd find him lying on the sofa watching TV, waiting for me to come home and cook him tea. I started to get resentful. Although we were arguing, I still loved him deeply.

After we had been there for about a year, the bottom dropped out of my world again—this time in a heart-breaking way.

I found a letter Mike had written to a work colleague, telling her that he couldn't stop thinking about her, how he didn't love me anymore and didn't fancy me. This was before the days of text and email and mobile phones, so a letter was the easiest way to try to get into her knickers!

I felt like I had been stabbed in the heart. I felt so hurt and betrayed. In my mind, I connected him saying he didn't fancy me to my weight, and that kick-started a 27-year battle with poor body image—something I still suffer from today (although I'm now working on it!).

Once again, I called my parents and asked them to get me. They arrived a week later with a moving van and moved me home, where I laid low for a while to lick my wounds.

I found out when I married him years later (yes, I know. What was I thinking?), that he never did send the letter and had regretted what happened for years. He did turn up at work one day and asked me to forgive him and try again, but I wasn't prepared to restore my trust in him.

WHOOPS ROUND 5: DOMESTIC VIOLENCE AGAIN

"You are braver than you believe, stronger than you seem, and smarter than you think." –Christopher Robin

A few months later, Caroline, my best friend from childhood, arrived home from living in London. We started some serious partying—clubbing two or three nights a week, drinking more than we should have, and losing count of the number of times we'd go straight to work the next morning after an all-nighter.

I met Bill on one of these nights out. Bill had been in the year above me at school and was the school heartthrob. He was funny, popular and charming and I was so flattered that he liked me! He made me feel beautiful and sexy, and we started a passionate and exciting relationship. For the first year or so, everything was wonderful.

He was a painter and decorator during the day and ran a part-time business as a mobile DJ at weekends. I would often tag along to the parties he was DJ'ing at, and we would have such a good time, drinking and laughing and taking the mickey out of the guests.

We could chat for hours and hours about anything. We would dream about what we wanted to do, trips we would take, where we would live. We were a rampant couple in our early twenties who both still lived at home, so our sex life usually involved the back of his car and a dark part of Dundry (a local place out in the countryside that was renowned for young lovers!).

We were spending all our time together, so we decided to move into a shared house with his best friend and my friend Caroline. At last, I felt I was settled. I felt cherished and safe. I have always been very open, so Bill knew what had happened in my two previous relationships and promised that he would never hurt me. I believed him. He would tell me how beautiful I was and how lucky he was. I was content, happy and excited to be in love.

Everybody loved Bill. He was everyone's mate. Happy-go-lucky. Charming. The life and soul of the party. Then the partying became a daily occurrence, and his drinking grew heavier and heavier. At first, he was a happy drunk—at least, he was in front of everyone. At home, though, he became a nasty drunk. He was jealous and didn't like me talking to other guys at the pub, accusing me of flirting.

After one night at the pub, he came home and hit me; he was drunk. I couldn't believe I was in this place again, and the realisation left me gutted. Was it me? He had never hit a girl before, so it must have been me. It was my fault. I must have pushed him too hard. I told myself all these things to rationalize what I had thought would never happen again.

Afterwards, he would sob and beg my forgiveness, telling me he loved me so much and it would never happen again. I was desperate to believe him, so I stayed and forgave him. Until the next time. And the next time.

Interestingly, after my first experience with domestic violence, I swore I would never allow someone to do that to me again. Yet here I was, forgiving him time after time.

My friend Caroline became the referee. I found out 20 years later that when she knew he was at the pub, she would sit on the end of her bed, waiting for him to come home so she could be there to stop him from hitting me. My heart broke when I heard that. I had been so wrapped up in my own misery; I never noticed the impact it had on her. She would fly out of her room and jump between us so he couldn't hurt me. I was, and still am, incredibly blessed to consider her my best friend.

Thank God for Dads

*"There are two primary choices in life: to accept conditions as they exist, or accept the responsibility for changing them." –*Dr. Denis Waitley

Things went from bad to worse. Bill went to the pub every night, pacing the house like a panther until it opened at 7pm. He started selling things to pay for drinks. I knew I needed to get out but didn't know how. Again, I felt trapped. The final straw came when he said he was going to sell my video player. I'm not sure why that tipped me over the edge, but it did.

I called my Dad (again) and told him what had been happening. I told him that Bill was violent and I was worried what he would do when he found out I wanted to leave him. Everything in the house was mine, from the furniture to the dishes, so I didn't want to leave it all there for Bill to sell. Dad told me not to worry, just to start packing and he would be there with some help. I told Caroline what I was doing, and when she told me a friend's mother was renting out a property, we decided to move in together there.

A Moonlight Flit

"You must take personal responsibility. You cannot change the circumstances, the seasons, or the wind, but you can change yourself." –Jim Rohn

Within an hour, Dad turned up with half a dozen mates, vans, and cars, and within 30 minutes, we had cleared the house of all my stuff. I was so grateful that they had come to help me.

I felt like a complete failure. I felt like an idiot. How the hell had I let myself get into these situations. Three relationships—two cases of domestic abuse and one cheater? I passionately believe that if it weren't for what happened next, my life would have spiralled downwards at a terrifyingly rapid pace.

MY "SLIDING DOOR" MOMENT

"Every choice you make has an end result." –Zig Ziglar

I started my working life in catering. Had I been passionately dreaming of being a chef since I was little, baking jam tarts and rock cakes at home? No, I hadn't. Like most people when they leave school I had absolutely no idea what I wanted to do with the rest of my life. I wasn't particularly interested in cooking, but my sister had gone to catering college, and they were having an open day. Myself, Caroline and another good friend, Cath (who also had no interest in cooking), went to the college open day so we could get a day off school.

Two years later the three of us graduated from catering college as fully trained (but still a bit clueless) chefs.

I was lucky enough to get a job as a Commis Chef in a fantastic banquet and conference centre in Bristol called Ashton Court Mansion. For those of you unfamiliar with the kitchen brigade, a Commis Chef is a posh word for general dogsbody. It's about as low as it gets.

Luckily for me, it was a small kitchen team, and as people left over the next couple of years, I was promoted. By the time I was 20 I had worked my way up to Sous Chef, which is the next one down from Head Chef.

Looking back now, if it hadn't been for my "sliding door" moment while I was a chef, I could have very well have stayed working in catering and living with abusive men my entire life.

N.B. In case you haven't seen the film, a "sliding door moment" is when a simple decision that doesn't seem particularly important at the time completely changes the direction of your life. Moments such as when you decided to go to that particular pub on that particular night and met your future husband or wife. Imagine how different your life would be if you'd gone to a different pub. Although for some of you that might be a pleasant thought.

My First Introduction to the Wonderful World of Personal Development

"Put all excuses aside and remember this: YOU are capable." – Zig Ziglar

When I was 20, I was introduced to the world of Network Marketing or MLM (Multi-level marketing). Although I didn't actually make any money, it completely changed my life. Deciding to join that MLM company was my "sliding door" moment. This one decision has had a huge impact on my life. Had I not signed up, I would have missed out on the countless incredible experiences I have had the opportunity to participate in since.

(By the way, I truly believe that picking up this book could be one of your "sliding door" moments.)

If you have ever been involved in the MLM industry, you will know that the MLM companies really push personal development. We had a "book of the month" and "tape of the week" programme, so at aged 20, I was reading books like *Think and Grow Rich* by Napoleon Hill, *The Magic of Thinking Big* by David J. Schwartz and *The Power of Your Subconscious*

Mind by Joseph Murphy.

What I learned completely changed my outlook on life. I started to dream about the life I wanted, and more importantly, I started to believe that it was possible.

My new positive mindset gave me the confidence to end the second abusive relationship. I wanted the cycle to stop before it became my life story. How often do we hear about women who lurch from one abusive relationship to another? I didn't want that to be me, so I ended the cycle. Or so I thought...

The Magic of Thinking Big

"There's a difference between interest and commitment. When you're interested in doing something, you do it only when circumstances permit. When you're committed to something, you accept no excuses, only results." –Unknown

When I was 20, the Head Chef left to go travelling, and our new Head Chef arrived. To be honest, although he was a lovely guy, he was a bit of a plonker. He would put paprika on the roast potatoes to make them look the right colour, rather than cooking them properly. I kid you not. He made mistake after mistake, and over time we started to lose our reputation as the best place to hold your wedding reception in Bristol.

I was halfway through reading *The Magic of Thinking Big* when I decided that I wanted his job. I knew I could do it better. The book gave me the confidence to go for the Head Chef position, something I wouldn't have dreamed of doing a year earlier. The management wasn't particularly keen, to be honest. There weren't too many female Head Chefs around in the late 80s, especially one that had only just turned 21!

My boss knew our reputation was suffering and that he had

to do something. I kept on at him to just give me a chance to prove myself. I offered to do a trial for six weeks for no extra pay, which swung it!

Eleven years later I was still there, thankfully with a few pay rises along the way. Although I loved my job, Ashton Court was a great place to work, and I had the same team with me for years, my eyes and mind had been opened to life's rich opportunities, and I was always on the lookout for another business opportunity.

Ambitious and determined to have a great life, I bought my first flat when I was 21. It was a 2-bed maisonette above a shop, so I rented out both the bedrooms and I used the living room as a bedroom. I worked an extra job in the video shop downstairs on my nights off to help pay the mortgage. My best friend had moved in with me, so we had a good few years of partying and clubbing. Life was good. On the surface.

SINGLE MOTHERHOOD

"Courage is simply the willingness to be afraid and act anyway." –Dr. Robert Anthony

Although my career was doing great, my personal life was not so good.

I still had a weight problem, and although the men in my life didn't seem to mind, I was very unhappy with myself.

Over the next few years, I seemed to stumble from one short-term relationship to another. I understand now that I was attempting to use sex to find love. For a while, I believed that a way to a man's heart was between the sheets. Or on top of them. Or in the back of a car. In a field!

One of these brief relationships led to me getting pregnant and at 25, I became a single mother to my wonderful daughter Abby. Not keeping her never crossed my mind. I felt that she was "meant to be". I had known her father for a few months –he was a work friend of Caroline's, and we would meet up when we were out drinking. He had separated from his wife and the only time I slept with him also happened to be "egg night" and the first time I had had sex in 2 years! What are the chances? As I said, she was definitely meant to be!

I was 25, I owned my own home, I had a good job and a good support network around me, so why wouldn't I? By the time I found out I was pregnant the guy had got back together with his wife and made it clear that he didn't want to be involved. I was fine with that, although I secretly hoped he would want to see Abby for her sake if not for his. Unfortunately, he never really did. He met her once and thought she was beautiful but was petrified that his wife would find out.

I used my pregnancy as an excuse to eat everything in sight and gained over five stone. Deep fried sweet and sour pork balls were not the healthiest craving to have and living a hundred yards from a great Chinese takeaway didn't help either.

My boss was great and let me work right up until Abby was born, as I couldn't afford to take maternity leave. She used to protest at being so close to big hot saucepans by giving me a big kick if she got too warm.

On the 5th January, Abby arrived into the world 11 days late at nearly 10 pounds (she obviously enjoyed the sweet and sour pork balls too!). My due date was Christmas Day, so I was glad she was late! I must say single motherhood was a shock to the system. I don't think anything fully prepares you for the absolute responsibility of a little person!

I was super organised and "on it" though. My years of being Head Chef in a busy banqueting centre had polished my planning and organisation skills until they were gleaming! I would lay out her clothes for the week in little piles on the dresser. And when I was on a late shift I would time the kettle to boil half an hour before I was due home, so the water was the perfect temperature to make her bottles when I got in! How organised is that?

My health visitor would arrive and joke that for someone considered "high risk" as a single mum – I looked better than she did! I was always up, dressed and looking reasonably smart with makeup on when she arrived.

Six weeks later I went back to work, which was one of the hardest things I have ever had to do. Luckily my lovely sister Aly was a childminder, so she could look after Abby for me. It meant that I missed many of her "firsts" but not working wasn't an option. Abby and I were a team. We developed the most beautiful bond – one that has stayed with us ever since.

Another Mike

When Abby was about one-year-old, I started dating a man from work. Also called Mike. At least I wasn't going to forget his name! Again, he was completely different to the type of guys I usually went for. My usual type were men with the bad boy twinkle in their eyes, and Mike Two was more of a safe guy, someone who I thought would be a good father to my daughter.

Marriage

Eighteen months later we had a huge white wedding at Ashton Court. If I am honest, I realised before we got married that he was not right for me, but I squashed that feeling and married him anyway.

And so began the eight years of our unhappy marriage.

Just a few months after we were married the memories started to surface…

WHOOPS ROUND 6: MEMORIES

"Obstacles don't have to stop you. If you run into a wall, don't turn around and give up. Figure out how to climb it, go through it, or work around it." –Michael Jordan

Crash! That was the sound of the bottom falling out of my world again. I started to get flashbacks about the abuse that had happened when I was a child. It was an awful time, and I now believe that the memories were triggered by having a man around my daughter.

For a while, I thought I was going mad. How could I have not known? Surely that couldn't have happened to me. I'd often cry for no reason at the most inappropriate times! I'd like to say that I dealt with it once and for all at this point in my life, but I didn't. I didn't want to talk about it or deal with it, so I buried it again and pretended everything was totally fine. In fact, I pretended that I was not only fine, I also pretended I was happy. No one would have ever known how unhappy I was.

Desperate for something to occupy my thoughts, we decided to have a baby. Just 11 months after making that decision, my beautiful son Sam was born. By now my memories were safely locked away for good. Hmmm, who was I kidding?! I continued with my bad habit of comfort eating, and within a year or so I had gained the six stone that I'd lost before my wedding. My excuse this time was that apart from all that "stuff" I hadn't dealt with, it was too hard because I was working with food all day and had to taste everything. It's amazing what excuses or reasons we can come up with.

Into the Personal Development Arena Again

"Life is 10% what happens to us and 90% how we react to it." – Dennis P. Kimbro

In the late 90s I was introduced to Network Marketing again. My husband and I ran it together, and this time, armed with the success principles I'd learned back when I was 20, we actually made quite a lot of money!

We were taken on all-expense paid trips all over the world to places like Australia and Malaysia, on a Caribbean cruise, to Monte Carlo, Barcelona, and Madeira. Wow, what an eye-opener that was. Gala dinners, posh frocks, fantastic food, sandy white beaches and staying up all night drinking with friends was a pretty great way to spend your time!

Once again, I was reading the same books, listening to the same tapes (well, they were CDs by now). I loved it. Life was good but only on the surface – I had gotten pretty good at ignoring my innermost thoughts and worries.

WHOOPS ROUND 7: MORE BULLYING

"Everyone faces defeat. It may be a stepping-stone or a stumbling block, depending on the mental attitude with which it is faced." –Napoleon Hill

Not only was I unhappy in my marriage, but I was also desperately unhappy with my weight, so I decided to do something about it once and for all. I started to do some serious work on myself. I was reading self-help books like they were going out of fashion. I was like a sponge. I wanted to understand why I could be so successful in my career and business but struggle to apply the same principles to my weight. I was so frustrated with myself. Why couldn't I resist the urge to eat?

I grew as a person both spiritually and emotionally and was turning into a successful businesswoman. Unfortunately, although my husband was reading the same books (and could quote them verbatim), he didn't seem to internalise what he was reading. He would spout off about positive thinking in front of our team and then be pessimistic and negative when we were at home. He started to pick at me about everything I did or said. If I said black, he said white. If I said yes, he said no. It was exhausting. Then he started to belittle me in front of our friends and family. This went on for years.

Over this time, I completely lost confidence in myself and was a shadow of the person that I was when I met him. I'd lost my sparkle. I now understand that he was just scared because he knew I was outgrowing him, so he did his utmost to keep me at his level.

I was depressed and despondent. Desperate to lose weight, I started smoking weed at night when the kids were in bed, kidding myself that it was better for me than alcohol as it didn't have any calories. Another habit that allowed me to block out the pain of having to deal with my "stuff" and take responsibility for my life.

By 2003, both the marriage and the business had pretty much fallen apart. We spent most of our time screaming at each other, arguing day and night, and had started to fall into debt. I couldn't see a way out. Our lives were so entangled in the business and our mounting debts that I didn't know what to do. I wanted to get out of the marriage for the kids more than anything. It was not a healthy environment.

ANOTHER "SLIDING DOOR" MOMENT

"You don't need someone to tell you what to do. You know what you need to do. Do it." –Randy Gage

One of my favourite authors at the time was a guy called Randy Gage. I loved his books, they were really motivating, and his words seemed to resonate with me. We heard that he was coming to London to do a prosperity seminar and I desperately wanted to go. We were massively in debt at this point and really couldn't afford it. Not only was it a struggle to find someone to look after the kids, our credit card bills were already enormous. To say we were living beyond our means is a bit of an understatement. If you've ever run your own business, you will understand that overheads are overheads, regardless of how much money you have coming in. Our overheads stayed the same, our turnover and profit didn't.

So, back to that "sliding door" moment. Usually, it was me that tried to put a brake on our spending, but this time for some reason, I said, "what the hell, let's put it on the credit card". I just knew that it was crucial that we went. This turned out to be a life-changing decision.

The seminar was good. I didn't hear much that I hadn't heard before, but this time something in me just clicked into place. At the very beginning, Randy Gage said that there were three types of people in the room. Those that would listen to what he said, think that it was interesting and do absolutely nothing with the information. Then there were those that would think it was great, be motivated to change, make some changes in the short term but be back in the same place in months (if not weeks). And then there was the last group, the minority. These people would go away and completely change their lives. I was in the last group. The thought of still being in the same place in six months' time was just plain terrifying. I knew that I had to take radical action. The rest of the seminar went by in a bit of a blur as I plotted and planned what I would do.

The first step was to face reality. And I mean really face reality. Not look at it through my usual positive, rose-tinted glasses. This is what I came up with:

- **The house was a complete mess.**

This wasn't an understatement. I was embarrassed when people came to the house. My husband was a decorator by trade, but you would have never believed it. Over the years, he had stripped the wallpaper from the hall, stairs, and landing, then not decorated it as he didn't have the time. When he did have the time, we didn't have the money for materials.

Then he decided to knock a wall down in the kitchen by whacking a sledgehammer through it and realised the wall was load bearing. He just left the hole. This turned into holes as throughout the rest of the afternoon, he and his builder mate "investigated" the kitchen. It stayed like that for months. Grrrr…

One day I asked him to trim the hedge at the front of the house while I was out for the day. When I came home the hedge had been given a "number one" and had gone from five foot to just under a foot. It looked a mess.

My son Sam had accidentally left the tap running full blast with the plug in the sink in the upstairs bathroom. Oops. The ceiling collapsed, and we were left with no ceiling. For months. And months.

- **We were about £30,000 in debt.**

- **Our outgoings were a lot higher than our incomings.**

- **Financially my husband wouldn't be able to support me.**

- **The business wasn't going to be able to support me.** Although there was still some income coming through it wasn't going to be anywhere near enough for what I needed. Running the business together was simply not going to work. We disagreed about everything.

- **I would be a single mother again, this time with two small kids.**

- **The kids would miss their father.** They were only six and nine at the time, and I knew that he wouldn't bother with them much when he left. He had three boys from a previous marriage that he only saw when I arranged it.

- **I didn't know how I was going to earn a living.**

- **I didn't have either childcare for the kids or anyone to watch them after school or during the holidays.**

- **I was extremely unfit and unhealthy.** I smoked 40 cigarettes a day, was still smoking dope at night, never exercised, drank only to get drunk, ate convenience crap and weighed over 220 pounds.

- **Things were NOT going to get better on their own.**

- **Making a change in six months or a year wasn't going to be any easier than it was going to be now.**

I realised that I owed it to myself and my kids to change my life now. I forced myself to hold up a mirror and see the truth about what life would be like if I stayed. It was a difficult exercise, but I made myself go there emotionally. I faced the fact that if I didn't change my life now, then we could lose the house. We really could end up homeless. I made myself think about how I would feel in five years' time if I was still unhappy, overweight and unhealthy.

As I said, it was a tough and challenging exercise, but I understood that I needed to get some leverage – to give me the courage and motivation to do what had to be done. For years, I had been saying to myself, "Things will get better soon", but this was just an excuse not to make the difficult changes. It was easier to stay in my marriage than to face the unknown. It was easier to be unhappy than to try and untangle our lives.

So, this was what was going through my mind as I was sat listening to Randy Gage. I made an internal commitment to myself that I was going to change things. Now. I was ready to change, and it had to be now.

The Drive Home

"Be willing to let go of who you are, to become who you might be." –Randy Gage

We were halfway through our two-hour journey home before

I plucked up the courage to tell him I wanted a divorce. I wanted to tell him before we got home to the kids, as I didn't want them to overhear us. It was one of the most difficult conversations that I had ever had. He just didn't see it coming. I thought he must have realised how bad things were, but he kept saying that things were not that bad, that we could work through it and that he loved me. We were both sobbing, so with hindsight having this conversation while we were driving was probably not the best idea in the world.

It's Funny How the Universe Works...

"In three words, I can sum up everything I've learned about life. It goes on." –Robert Frost

The next few months were horrendous. We were still living together, working together and sleeping in the same bed. I think he was hoping that he could change my mind, which he nearly did a few times. I spent most of the time crying and trying to work out how I was going to cope. What could I do for work? Where would he live? I couldn't just throw him out on the street.

Then I had a call that enabled me to see the shimmer of light at the end of the tunnel. For years, I'd rented out the flat that I had bought when I was 21 to long-term renters, and one day the tenants called to say they wanted to move out as they were going to buy their own place. I felt like a massive weight had been lifted off my shoulders. I could see a way out – I'd just give him the flat. I'd keep the house, and as it was only half a mile down the road, it would be handy for the kids.

Eventually, after another month or so, he moved out. I was left with no job, no business as such, a house that was falling down around me, £30,000 worth of debt, two small kids to look after and a wee bout of depression! Not the best time in my life to be honest.

Rather than moping around having a pity party, I picked myself up, dusted myself off and went in search of a new life. I applied the success principles that I had learned over the years. Goal-setting, affirmations, positive thinking. I was on it! I made a plan to find a new career, give up smoking, get myself healthy and become debt free as quickly as I could. I was on a mission.

First, I re-mortgaged the house, fixed up everything that needed fixing and redecorated from top to bottom.

Next, I started one of those daft liquid and bar diets and lost 96 pounds in six months. (This didn't turn out to be my best move, as within two years I ended up gaining it all back again – with an extra 30 pounds on top!)

In the last month of dieting, I decided to quit smoking 40 cigarettes a day, which I did with the help of hypnotherapy, and after I'd lost about three stones, I even started to go to the gym on a regular basis. I was feeling incredibly proud of myself at this point. Life was good, I felt good, I looked good, and my career was taking off.

BUSINESS SUCCESS!

"Don't wait until everything is just right. It will never be perfect. There will always be challenges, obstacles and less than perfect conditions. So what. Get started now. With each step you take, you will grow stronger and stronger, more and more skilled, more and more self-confident and more and more successful." –Mark Victor Hansen

So, here I was. Divorced, two kids, no job or business and a husband that couldn't support me. I started hunting on the job sites to find something that paid well that I could do around the kids.

I took on a self-employed, commission-only sales job selling advertising. I had never had any formal sales training, didn't have a clue what I was doing and lucky for me, nobody told me that advertising was one of the hardest things in the world to sell. I would sit in the car before going into an appointment literally shaking with fear. I would give myself a virtual slap around the face, sit quietly and visualise a positive outcome to the meeting. I would imagine how great I would feel when I left the meeting with a sale in my hand. I started listening to positive CDs in the car when I was driving from appointment to appointment. Thank God for Zig Ziglar and Tony Robbins.

This was the start of a very lucrative and successful career in sales. Since then, career-wise I have been successful at whatever I put my mind to, which I totally put down to what I learned from the hundreds of books I read, CDs I listened to and seminars I attended. I have always been a massive believer in the law of attraction and believe that the universe always has my back. Great opportunities kept flowing my way, and I never had a shortage of good prospects and clients.

I felt I was ready to date again but since my days of clubbing were over, I didn't know how or where I was going to meet someone. So I joined my first dating site. This was back when internet dating was just kicking off, so it was fun and flattering for a while. I just used to talk to people at first – too nervous to actually meet someone.

I started talking to a Yorkshire-man called Lee who lived in Scotland, thinking he was far enough away to be safe if I didn't want to meet him. It turns out Scotland is only 30 minutes away on a cheap EasyJet flight! Not quite as far away as I thought. We spoke on the phone for hours at a time over 3 or 4 weeks, and by the time he flew down to visit, I think we both knew we had to find a way to make it work.

He was confident, like-minded, ambitious and charming. Looking back, I think he was a narcissist, but I couldn't see it then. He definitely had the bad boy twinkle. He moved to Bristol, and we even set up in business together as he was also in sales.

I wish I could say this had a happy ending, but it didn't. He cheated on me. More than once. And I stupidly took him back. For him, it was about the sex, and I lost count of how many times he had cheated. I almost became immune to being hurt. Mainly because of my low self-esteem and low self-worth. My track record with men was dreadful. When things went wrong in my relationships, I honestly thought it was my fault.

That I didn't deserve anything better.

I eventually ended the relationship after four years, mainly because his relationship with Abby was awful. He was very strict, and I am pretty laid-back, so Abby rebelled against him when he came to live with us. It was like living in a war zone. It was horrible. I was constantly trying to keep the peace between them. They argued over everything, and he was so used to having his own way that he didn't know how to communicate with her. We had moved to Yorkshire to be closer to his daughters, but after a year I packed up and moved the kids back to Bristol.

Once again, I picked myself up, dusted myself off and started again, this time swearing that I was giving up on men and relationships!

The Universe Always Delivers

"See the things that you want as already yours. Know that they will come to you at need. Then let them come. Don't fret and worry about them. Don't think about your lack of them. Think of them as yours, as belonging to you, as already in your possession." –Robert Collier

In 2006 I moved back to Bristol and was lucky enough to find a wonderful little house in the street next to my parents. I was back in the area that I grew up in, and my children went to the same schools that I went to.

Selling to small businesses made me realise that many business owners didn't really know how to run a business properly. For example, a good plumber starts a business because he is a good plumber, not because he is a good businessman. As the business grows, he finds himself doing much less of the thing he loves (i.e. plumbing) and far more of the things he hates and doesn't know how to do, i.e. tasks like budgets, cash-flow forecasts, and marketing plans.

So, in 2007 I invested in a Business Coaching franchise and trained to become an ActionCOACH.

Finding ActionCOACH

I can remember sitting on my sofa one Sunday evening after a particularly stressful week. I had driven over 1,000 miles and worked an average of 13 hours a day for the previous 14. I was knackered.

I looked up to the universe and said: "I want to find a way to halve my hours, double my income and love what I do with a passion." That was it. No specifics. I didn't mind what I did. I was more than happy to leave it to the universe! The very next day, a franchise called ActionCOACH came at me from three different directions. I was talking on the phone with an old friend, and she told me she had just started working with an ActionCOACH. I had an email about the franchise opportunity, and later in the afternoon, I had a random call from their sales office asking if I was interested in talking with them. I have a deal with the universe that if something comes onto my radar three times in quick succession, I am supposed to take a good look. So, I did. And the franchise fitted me like a glove. It was exactly what I was looking for.

Joining ActionCOACH was another one of my great decisions. I was back into the personal development arena. This time I was nagging my clients to read the same books that I had been reading for 20 years. I loved being an ActionCOACH, it is a great franchise, and over the years I have had some fantastic clients, many of whom turned into great friends.

MARRIAGE NUMBER TWO TO MIKE NUMBER ONE

"I would rather attempt something great and fail than attempt to do nothing and succeed." –Robert Schuller

In 2009 I met up with Mike One again. Damn that pesky Facebook! A mutual friend had added me, and stupidly I sent him a message asking how he was. I hadn't seen him for over 20 years, and I was curious as to what he was up to. He messaged me straight back, and that was the start of weeks of messages. He kept asking me out for a drink, and I kept refusing. He told me how sorry he was, how stupid he'd been and how he had regretted what he had done every day since.

Eventually, I agreed to meet him for a drink. It was like putting on an old pair of slippers! We got on brilliantly and chatted for hours. He asked me to try again, but I refused. He asked again. I refused again. And again. I'll give him one thing – he was very persistent. After being "wooed" for months, I agreed to give him another chance, on the understanding that if he ever cheated on me, our relationship would be instantly over. No discussion. He swore he had learned his lesson and that he never wanted to lose me again.

The next year was wonderful. It was amazing how quickly we slipped back into how we were before things started going wrong. He asked me to marry him while we were sat watching the sunset on a beautiful beach in Majorca and we got married on Cocoa Beach in Florida a year later. I was a happy girl. Life was good. On the surface. I still hadn't dealt with my "stuff".

My career was also doing amazingly well, I was earning twice the average monthly income every week, but unfortunately, I failed to apply the success principles I'd learned in one key area of my life. My health. I was massively overweight, always stressed and a workaholic who took no exercise whatsoever.

It totally frustrated me that I seemed to be able to apply what I'd learned over the years to just about every area of my life except my weight. It drove me mad. For years. I lost weight. I gained weight. I lost weight. I gained weight. I started a diet. I blew my diet. I started a diet. I blew my diet. Over and over and over again. It was absolute madness.

I decided enough was enough and I set out on a mission to work out what was going on in my brain to make me sabotage myself over and over. I felt that I owed it to my clients. How could I coach them to improve their lives and businesses if I couldn't get in control of my weight?

LIFE IS A MIRROR

"Life is a mirror and will reflect back to the thinker what he thinks into it." –Ernest Holmes

Life has a funny way of showing you things that you need to take notice of. In my coaching practice, I started to notice the same self-sabotage in some of my clients. Some of them were not just sabotaging their weight loss and exercise programmes but were constantly procrastinating, and failing to make positive changes in other areas as well. For some of them, this was then leading to a lack of self-belief in their abilities to change and resulted in lower self-esteem.

Over the years, I learned that the key to happiness and success wasn't about the right strategy, it was about the right mindset. For example, many of the business owners I worked with were lousy at time management. I learned the hard way that I could teach them every time-management technique in the book, but if they didn't commit to action, nothing would ever change. And they had to be ready to change. Ready to take responsibility for their own behaviour.

Typically, they would flit from task to task muttering about how there were just not enough hours in the day and how they could never get on top of things, however hard they tried.

There may have been some short-term results, but they would always be back to square one within weeks. This was because they changed their external behaviour but didn't change their internal programming. Their subconscious mind had no choice other than to keep running the same original programme – "I am rubbish at time management".

I now believe, without a shadow of a doubt, that this is the key reason why most people struggle to make long-term changes. Some 98% of people who lose weight will gain it back again. They change their external behaviour, i.e. they go on a diet or start a healthy eating programme, but they don't change the way that they think about their ability to lose weight and keep it off. It's the same reason why over 90% of lottery winners will end up back where they started within five years. We will cover this in a lot more detail in later chapters.

So, this is where I was in January 2012. Overweight, unhealthy, working far too hard and spending most of my spare time either being fascinated by the brain and why we do what we do or fretting about my weight.

Our Internal Early Warning Alarm System

"Look within... The secret is inside you." –Hui-Neng

Now I believe that life has a way of trying to get our attention when we are off track. It starts with a tug in your tummy, a feeling that all is not well, but unfortunately most of us are excellent at ignoring it. It's our early warning system. We know things are not quite right, either in our jobs, career, business, health or relationships, but it's easier to stick our heads in the sand than deal with our "stuff". Stuff is messy and hard and may hurt. Denial, by the way, is not a river in Egypt... it's a dangerous place to be.

I was certainly in denial. I ignored the tugs and carried on my merry way.

So, if we ignore the tugs, life starts to tap you on the shoulder. These taps are a little more persistent, much harder to ignore and often come in the form of health, career, business or relationship problems.

For me, it was health problems and relationship problems. I had constant headaches. I woke up with one and went to bed with one and popped more painkillers than I care to think about. I allowed this to go on for four years. Seriously, four years.

I made a couple of token visits to the doctor's, only to be told that it was probably tension headaches. Excuse my language, but I felt like saying "No shit Sherlock" to the doctor who was treating me. I was working 70 plus hours a week, I was the main breadwinner in the family, which was a huge pressure, and had two teenage kids. Of course I was stressed.

My second marriage was on the rocks by now – we argued constantly, and I knew it wasn't right. We argued mainly about our kids. Either my son or his son. Mike was also a shouter – something that drove me to distraction. He would fly off the handle quickly and start yelling. I swore that I wouldn't live like that again, so I would try my best to keep calm which seemed to wind him up even more. Eventually, I would flip too, and we would start shouting at each other. Not good.

We were also just too different in too many ways. I am a dreamer, creative and driven. An entrepreneur who loves to take chances, have new experiences, and who lives life to the full. I was a doer, and Mike was more of a watcher. A steady

Eddie who didn't like change. He craved security and stability. With hindsight, it was never going to work.

Back in denial, once again I carried on doing what I was doing. Which was dieting or bingeing, working too many hours, popping headache pills and never – and I mean never – exercising.

So, we ignore the tugs, we ignore the taps and then life decides that enough is enough. It whacks you around the head with a baseball bat, throws you a curveball or the bottom drops out of your world. Things start to get serious and you either lose your job, your business or career, your relationship or your health.

WHOOPS ROUND 8: CANCER

"Cancer is a word, not a sentence." –John Diamon

For me, that curveball came in the form of cancer. Breast cancer to be more specific. I was in the bath one day in early January, and as I was washing, I felt a lump on the side of my right breast. It was big. Enormously big. And I knew. I felt this icy realisation that I had cancer. Nothing that big should be there. I made an appointment to see the doctor that day at emergency surgery, and the look on the doctor's face gave it away. She tried to sound calm and told me that we would "get it checked out, just to be on the safe side", but her face told a very different story. She looked petrified... A little like a bunny caught in the headlights. Bless her.

Waiting for the appointment for the breast clinic over the next two weeks were two of the longest weeks of my life. I tried to stay positive but I already knew I had cancer, so my practical brain kicked in and I started to think through my options. I just had to carry on working.

As I was running my own business, taking a year out was simply not an option. I had to find a way to carry on working. I started searching the breast cancer forums for people that worked through chemo. This happened to be the absolute worst thing I could have done. Do not ever, EVER, go near these forums if you want to stay positive. It's full of hundreds of lovely people who seem to get relief from describing each side effect in minute detail. Yikes. This was not the place for me. "Out of sight, out of mind" was my motto in those days.

Back in my early MLM days I read a brilliant Mark Twain quote in a book called *Being Happy* by Andrew Matthews:

"I've been through some terrible things in my life, SOME of which actually happened!"

Love it. How profound is that?

Our minds have a terrible habit of exploring the "what ifs" – taking us to these dark and dismal places where the absolute worst happens.

A client once told me the following story. We'd been working together for a while, and she was learning how to get in control of her thinking. She hadn't been getting on with her partner for a while, and one evening he was late coming home from work.

She said...

In an instant, I went from "He's late" to...

"I wonder where he is...

He didn't look very happy this morning...

Perhaps he is going off me...

In fact, he hasn't complimented me for a while...

Can't remember the last time we had sex either...

What if he is with someone else...

That girl at his work is beautiful and has a fantastic figure...

Perhaps he is with her...

She's single I think...

Much slimmer than me...

They could have stopped for a drink on the way home...

Oh my God...I think he could be having an affair...

It's because I have gained a few pounds...

He doesn't fancy me anymore...

He is going to leave me...

WTF? Why do we do that? And the scary thing is that this whole conversation happened in my head in an instant. I only just managed to stop myself from throwing his clothes out of the bedroom window.

Eventually, he walked up the path, weary from his day and pissed at missing his train, not realising how close he'd come to being greeted by a pile of boxer-shorts, his favourite CDs, and his 'loving girlfriend' about to launch at him all guns blazing. Thank goodness, I realised what I was doing and calmed down."

Seriously... why do we do that?

What an absolute waste of time and energy! Really... it is. We create these awful situations and let our imaginations run wild. Well, stop it!

I didn't want to think about all the terrible things that "might happen" so made a conscious decision that I was not going to allow my mind to go there. Thinking I was going to die from cancer was not going to help me at this point, so I refused to allow my mind to go there. Lots on how to do that in Part Two.

The Breast Clinic

"We have two options, medically and emotionally: give up or fight like hell." –Lance Armstrong

Eventually, after what seemed like an age, but was actually only a couple of weeks, my appointment came through for the breast clinic. In the UK, you go and have all your tests and wait around for the results, which is better than waiting for weeks.

The doctor arrived at 5pm with a sombre face and told me that yes, unfortunately, it was cancer. The lump was nearly nine centimetres in diameter, about the size of a small orange. Another WTF – how the hell had I missed that for goodness sake? You'd think I would have noticed that, wouldn't you?

Was I checking myself regularly like we all know we should? No, I wasn't. I would have a general feel around now and then, but it was very hit or miss. In my defence, I had lost a couple of stone before Christmas, so I am putting it down the fact that losing the extra weight made the lump easier to find but... I should have been checking.

Looking back now I realised that I had a massive case of "white coat syndrome". This dude had a white coat on, and he told me what was going to happen, so that's what was going to happen. I didn't question what he had to say. My Mum had been the same. If her doc had said the sky was pink today, then the sky was pink. End of story. As I mentioned earlier, I had suffered a lot with chest infections when I was a kid, so I was very used to going to the doctor to get "fixed". It didn't cross my mind that there could have been another, maybe better, way to treat my cancer other than to poison it, cut it out or burn it.

I was told I was going to have six rounds of chemo, followed by surgery and then possibly radiotherapy. My husband was in shock, more so than me as I had already started to come to terms with it in my own mind. There was no sobbing or hysterics like you sometimes see on the television, and I didn't drop to my knees and start wailing "Why me, why me". It was quite surreal looking back. It was all rather emotionless and matter of fact.

Telling My Family

The ultimate measure of a man is not where he stands in moments of comfort and convenience, but where he stands at a time of challenge and controversy." –Dr. Martin Luther King Jr.

I have always been the strong one. The one that my friends came to for help. That "Happy Jo" persona I had built when I was in my teens had stayed with me and I never really allowed myself to be the vulnerable one. Telling friends and family was not something I was looking forward to. We drove straight to my Mum and Dad's house to tell them first, and I will never forget the look of devastation in my Mum's eyes when I told her I had cancer. She had lost a dear friend to cancer, so knew only too well how this could possibly end. I told her that we had to stay positive and strong and that I was going to be fine. I didn't allow myself to cry while I was there even though I wanted nothing more than for her to hug me and tell me not to worry and that everything was going to be fine. It was a while before I allowed myself to cry.

Next were my kids. By now they were 15 and 18, so grown up enough to understand what cancer was all about. My son seemed to take it in his stride and went back to playing his Xbox shortly afterwards (as only teenage boys can do) but my daughter Abby was a different story. She was totally devastated and sobbed uncontrollably despite my best efforts to reassure her that I was going to be fine. That was the hardest part... Abby and I had always had a fiery but extremely close relationship, and I don't think I had fully understood how hard it was going to hit her. Next on my list was my lovely sister Aly who was also devastated but stayed strong for me.

I decided to call some of my friends and let the rest know by text. Sounds a bit odd looking back but I was already fed up with telling people and hearing the sympathy and pity in their voices. So thank goodness for text messages and Facebook Messenger. I wrote a message to everyone telling them what had happened, that I was going to be fine and that they were to treat me exactly the same. I banned them all from giving me the head to the side, puppy-dog-eyed "How are you feeling?" speech. The best response I had was from one of my lovely clients whose wife was just finishing treatment for breast cancer. "For fuck's sake" just about summed it up!

I found out much later that some of those closest to me had sobbed to their partners when they got my message or call. They were all strong and positive in front of me though for which I was very grateful.

There were many times during my treatment when I could have allowed my mind to take me down some dark and dismal places but for the most part, I was able to keep in control of my thinking. I watched funny videos on YouTube, watched comedy films or binged on box sets to keep my mind busy and distracted. I used NLP (Neuro-Linguistic Programming) and CBT (Cognitive Behaviour Therapy) and drew on just about every tool in my resilience toolbox to get through the next year or so. If you are not sure what those are, don't worry – I will explain them all later.

Chemo

"You can be a victim of cancer or a survivor of cancer. It's a mindset." –Dave Pelzer

Chemo is shit. There really is no way to dress it up. It is what is it. Poison being pumped around your body, killing not only cancer cells but many other perfectly healthy cells too. Nothing can prepare you for it. You know how it feels to have the type of flu where you can't get out of bed? Where everything hurts? Well, times that by 100 and that's what "chemo" week was like. I was told I was going to have six rounds in a three-week cycle.

I was lucky enough to have chemo at home, so I didn't have to go and sit in oncology with all the sick-looking people. The nurse would arrive on a Friday morning, attach the drip and sit with me for a couple of hours while the chemo was dripped into my veins.

Chemo can damage your veins quickly, so it got harder and harder for the nurse to find a vein. After my second chemo, I had a "port" put straight into my heart to make it easier. The next nine days became known as "chemo week", where even walking up the stairs would leave me so exhausted that I would often just sit on the bed and cry. I cried a lot during chemo weeks.

Losing My Hair

"You gain strength, courage, and confidence by every experience in which you really stop to look fear in the face. You must do the thing which you think you cannot do." –Eleanor Roosevelt

I started to lose my hair after my second chemo. For me, this was one of the hardest things about the whole journey. Finding clumps of hair on my pillow every morning was devastating. I can remember gently washing my hair in the bath one day, and I could feel it coming away in my hands. I was so shocked at the amount of hair in the bath as I emptied it, that I sat on the floor and cried. Like I said... I cried a lot in chemo week. I called my hairdresser and had her come shave it all off after that. I had already chosen my wig and had been slightly obsessive about buying as many different types of head coverings as I could, so I was ready. I hated what I looked like without hair, but for me, it was better than the daily stress of watching it fall out.

Side Effects

"You never know how strong you are until being strong is the only choice you have." –Cayla Mills.

As discussed, chemo is shit. The side effects were numerous and not something I am going to focus on too much in case anyone reading is about to embark on their own "dance with cancer". For me, the worst ones were the constant nausea and terrible mouth ulcers. At one point I was taking 26 different pills, lotions and potions to counteract the side effects from the chemo. Jeez, what was I thinking? My poor body. My hourly mantra became... "This too will pass". I knew that even though I felt like absolute crap, within a few days, I would start feeling human again.

I was lucky enough to find the Penny Brohn Cancer Care centre who offered a holistic approach to cancer treatment that included raw healthy vegan foods, exercise, meditation and mindfulness. I would like to say that I started eating healthily at this point, but I didn't. The doctor said not to worry about my weight for now, so I decided to take his advice. I regained the two stone I had lost before I found the lump, so I was the only person I know that actually gained weight when they had cancer. Damn those pesky steroids.

My Son

"Within you right now is the power to do things you never dreamed possible. This power becomes available to you just as soon as you can change your beliefs." –Dr. Maxwell Maltz

Although my lovely son looked like he was handling it all well on the outside, he started to get into trouble at school, so I knew he wasn't. I can remember being on the phone to his teacher while the nurse was injecting me with chemo. He had flipped out at school and walked out, and they couldn't find him. That was a pretty tough day and was the start of some difficult times with him. It's easy to forget how much cancer treatment impacts everyone around you sometimes. It was heart-breaking watching him suffer. I loved him with all my heart and was so sorry that he had to see me go through that.

Changing the Goalposts

"The human spirit is stronger than anything that can happen to it." –C.C. Scott

The side effects of chemo accumulate, so after each session, it was becoming harder and harder to bounce back quite so quickly. By the fourth round, I had had enough. My lovely client, whose wife had gone through the same treatment, kept telling me that I just needed to get through the next one because the last one didn't count. I thought, "Hey, that's a good belief to have", so I started telling myself every day, "Last one doesn't count. I'm nearly there". It became one of my daily mantras along with "This too will pass" and "The universe has my back".

One day, just after my fifth round, the oncologist just dropped into conversation, "Oh, didn't we tell you? We are going to give you eight rounds rather than six?"

WTF? In an instant, I had gone from being nearly done to only being just over halfway through. I was devastated. Absolutely gutted. That was one of the lowest moments of my treatment, and I did allow myself a good ole pity party over that one.

Faking It Until You Feel It

"People often say that motivation doesn't last. Well, neither does bathing – that's why we recommend it daily." –Zig Ziglar

As discussed, not working was simply not an option. I downsized my business, and the plan was to see my clients in my two "good" weeks. I deliberately scheduled a client coaching call for 8.30am the Monday after my "chemo week". Sometimes, I would have to literally drag myself out of bed and down to my conservatory, where I had set up my business after my diagnosis.

I would sit at my desk, give myself a pep talk, put on my "happy coach" hat and pick up the phone with a cheery, "Hi Paul, how was your weekend?" (as no one likes a mopey coach). By the end of that call, I was buzzing. It really was a case of fake it until you feel it. Neither your brain or your body knows the difference between real and make-believe. Forcing myself to be upbeat and positive for half an hour set me up for the rest of the day, and set the tone for the next two weeks. Yes, I had my down days, and I had to take it easy not to tire myself out too much, but generally, I felt good over those two weeks. Then it would all start again with the next round.

My husband, family, and friends were my absolute rocks throughout my treatment. From supportive simple text messages, surprise flower deliveries, free reiki healing sessions and home-cooked meals, to help with ironing and cleaning the house – it was all incredibly helpful. I was so very touched and grateful that so many wonderful people had my back.

After my seventh chemo, I had another MRI to check the size of the lump. Unfortunately, although the oncologist felt that the chemo had killed the cancer, it hadn't reduced the size of the lump, so I was still going to need a mastectomy. Again, I was absolutely gutted. Every day I had been visualising the doctor telling me that the lump had disappeared and I wouldn't need a mastectomy. But it didn't work... My surgery was scheduled for a few weeks later on the 5th September. Fuck!

My Surgery

"Take care of your body. It's the only place you have to live." – Jim Rohn

I have always had quite big boobs, so the thought of being without one, even for a while, was just awful. I opted for an immediate reconstruction. They were going to take muscle and fat from my back, move it around under my arm and use it to make a breast. It was a seven-hour operation which I wasn't looking forward to at all!

I suffer from low blood pressure, especially after an anaesthetic, so they kept me in recovery for a few hours longer, during which time I coached my nurse on her marital problems. I just can't help myself!

I stayed in the hospital for five days and was sent home with strict instructions to rest up and allow my reconstruction to "take".

WHOOPS ROUND 9: LOSING MY BEAUTIFUL MUM

"Bad things do happen; how I respond to them defines my character and the quality of my life. I can choose to sit in perpetual sadness, immobilized by the gravity of my loss, or I can choose to rise from the pain and treasure the most precious gift I have – life itself." –Walter Anderson

On Sunday, two days after I came home from the hospital, my husband cooked a delicious Sunday lunch for my parents and me. It was lovely to be home and eat some decent food. Little did I know that this would be the last time I would have a conversation with my Mum. Just as we were finishing up, Mum started to feel sick. She just about managed to get to the bathroom before she started vomiting. She was being sick for ages and Dad only just managed to get her home.

At first, we just thought it was a sickness bug, so I was told to stay away as my immune system was still pretty low due to the chemo. Over the next couple of days, she got worse, so Dad called the emergency doctor out. She had dehydrated quickly and was rushed into intensive care. Within hours she had slipped into a coma.

Looking back now it was all a bit of a blur. Rather than resting, I was up and down to Bristol Royal Infirmary to see her. I also had trouble with my wound. I had an infection, and my drains had fallen out, so I had to go to have my wounds drained. Most days I was on the fifth floor seeing my breast care nurse before going downstairs to see Mum in ICU. I was in agony. I hadn't quite prepared myself for how painful it was going to be.

I had my follow up appointment with my surgeon about a week after Mum was admitted to hospital. He said he felt that he had got clear margins when he removed the cancer and was confident that it was gone but still wanted to do radiotherapy to make sure we got rid of any remaining cancer cells. I went downstairs to tell Mum, thinking that she may still be able to hear me even through her coma. Miraculously, she woke up for long enough for me to tell her. She was very confused and couldn't talk, but I could see in her eyes that she understood me. Her eyes widened, and she smiled at me with her eyes.

We thought she was on the mend. She wasn't. We left the hospital full of hope only to be called back. She had another infection, and her internal organs were shutting down, and there was nothing they could do for her. They recommended that we come in and be ready to say our goodbyes. That was pretty much the worst moment of my life. She was fine. I didn't want to say goodbye for goodness sake. We were just having lunch. How the hell had this happened? But we had to let her go. As hard as it was, it wasn't fair. A machine was keeping her alive and looking at her I felt that she had already gone.

My husband, sister, brother-in-law, dad, son, and daughter gathered around her bed and said our goodbyes. We watched as the nurses turned off the life support and waited with her as she took her last breaths shortly after. It was heart-breaking. We were all in the most dreadful shock. At this point, we didn't even know why she died. I went into a panic thinking that she had caught my infection and that it was my fault, but the doctor gently assured me that this wasn't the case. He said she had died of pancreatitis, which still didn't make much sense to us as Mum wasn't a drinker, and pancreatitis is often associated with heavy drinking.

As the strong one, I went into practical mode and helped my Dad and sister to plan the funeral. The funeral was beautiful and was standing room only. My Mum was a beautiful soul. Everyone loved her. She was always cheerful and smiling, and always had time for you. I was extremely lucky to have her as my Mum.

My brave daughter Abby also wrote a beautiful poem for her Nan which she recited at the funeral. It was just so lovely. I don't know how she managed to keep it together. She was given a massive round of applause afterwards. I was so proud of her strength at such a terribly sad time.

Life Goes On

Once again, I picked myself up, dusted myself off and got on with life. We all missed Mum dreadfully, but life does go on. By now we knew my reconstruction hadn't worked and I was left with a shrivelled hard lump where my breast should have been. I had infection after infection, and three months later I was still having wound treatment. They had to delay my radiotherapy until my wound healed, so that was scheduled for January 2013.

My Mum

They say that hearts don't break, God, But that's not always true.
The day you took our Mum away,
You broke our hearts in two.
Look around your garden Lord,
She won't be hard to find,
She has a face that's full of love
And a heart that's good and kind.
Tell that we love her
And when you see her smile,
Put your arms around her
And hold her for a while!

I miss you so much Mum xxx.

(Poet unknown. I have searched high and low for the wonderful poet that created this beautiful poem but haven't been unable to find who wrote it.)

WHOOPS ROUND 10: CHEATING HUSBANDS

"Nothing hurts more than being disappointed by the single person you thought would never hurt you." –Unknown

In January 2013, I started radiotherapy. That was nowhere near as bad as chemo. It was just a nuisance having to go to the hospital every day for three weeks. By February I had finished my radiotherapy and was finally feeling like I was getting my life back on track.

I had watched a documentary over Christmas about the health benefits of the 5/2 way of eating. You eat normally for five days and for two days you only have 500 calories. The documentary said that on your 500 calorie "fasting" days, your body spends more time healing as it didn't have to worry about digesting food. It sounded perfect for me, so I thought I would give it a go. From day one I found it simple, effortless and easy and followed this way of eating for years – losing over 100 pounds. I never felt like I was on a diet.

By March, I had lost over 30 pounds and had gotten some of my energy back. I started to feel relatively normal again. I still missed Mum terribly and was still in pain, but I was starting to feel stronger. Unfortunately, Mike and I were not getting on and were always arguing or rowing.

Then the bottom dropped out of my world again. I found out he was having an affair.

Cancer, losing Mum and a cheating husband – all within the space of a year. You couldn't make this stuff up, could you? And I found out for sure on Mother's Day. Cue EastEnders theme tune (for any non-Brits reading this, EastEnders is one of those TV soaps where terrible things happen pretty much every day).

I can pinpoint the day that it had started. For about three weeks his mobile phone had been glued to his hand. He never put it down and never left it unattended, while before he would leave it all over the house. I can remember asking him one day whether he was doing something that he shouldn't be doing. He just laughed and said of course not.

Once a week, I drove a couple of hours to work with a large client, and usually we would book an apartment the night before so I could get an early start. He always came with me. He always said he wanted to make sure I was safe and that everything was OK. It also allowed us a "child-free" evening together which was nice. Suddenly he didn't want to come anymore and started to make excuses as to why he couldn't come. The last time he came, we ended up having the biggest row we had ever had which ended with me saying something along the lines of "Why don't we just get a divorce?" He said he didn't want to do that and we made up. Sort of. It felt a little like a temporary repair job, to be honest.

I knew something was going on, but it took me another week to prove it. His phone never left his side, and he had changed his password on his Facebook so I couldn't have a nose about.

After this had been going on for about three weeks, Caroline and her husband invited us to watch some live music at their local pub. The pub was out in the middle of nowhere, and I could never get a signal on my phone when we were there.

We all had our phones out on the table during the break, so I asked if I could borrow his phone as mine didn't have a signal and grabbed it before he had a chance to respond. His face told me all I needed to know. His face went as white as sheet, and he started to get stroppy, asking why I needed to use his phone and how he felt I was rude being on the phone in front of our friends.

I didn't need to look at his phone after that. His response was enough. I felt that familiar icy feeling of betrayal. I thought I was going to be sick. I handed it back and sat back to watch the second half of the gig, just wishing that I could leave right then but not wanting to cause a scene. We barely spoke when we got home. He knew that I knew and I wasn't quite ready to confront him, so we went to bed with an uneasy silence.

The next morning was Mother's Day. He was up early and said he was going to visit his Mum. I was cooking Sunday lunch for the family as it was the first Mother's Day since we'd lost Mum and we'd invited Dad over. As soon as he left, I went over to his computer and started searching through the browser history. I couldn't get onto his Facebook, but as I searched the browser history, I saw a snippet of a Facebook message sent that morning to someone called Cindy that said:

"Babe, we need to talk xxxxxxxxxxxxxxxxxxxxxxxx."

Who knew that you could still see snippets of your message history even when you are signed out of FB? I certainly didn't, and I guess Mike didn't either. I then searched "Cindy" and found another message on Valentine's day – just a simple *"xxxxxxxxxxxxxxxxxxxx"* Not very inventive as far as Valentine's messages go, but I got the picture.

He came home just after and I calmly asked who Cindy was. I could see from the look on his face that he was frantically trying to work out how much I knew. "Err... an old friend," he replied cautiously. "And...?" I prompted. It turns out he had hooked up with an old flame via Facebook (who was also married) and had been shagging her in the back of his car. How lovely!

I was devastated when I first found out. He betrayed me when I was at my most vulnerable. I hadn't recovered from losing Mum; I was still weak from chemo, surgery had left me with a mangled breast and an arm that I could hardly move. Oh, and I didn't have any hair.

Needless to say, I kicked him out. I found out at 12pm, and he was gone by 4pm. As he nearly cheated on me once before, he knew that once the trust was gone for me, that was it. Looking back, I think he wanted to get caught because he knew I would end it. He wouldn't have left me at this point, however bad things got because deep down, he was a decent guy – which may sound like an odd thing to say after he did what he did.

I don't feel any anger towards him at all now. At the time I did but looking back our marriage was on the rocks before I was diagnosed with cancer. He was an absolute rock for most of my treatment. Now I believe that he was brought back into my life to look after me during my treatment and once my treatment was over the universe wanted me to let him go because he wasn't right for me. I will always be grateful for the way he looked after me. Yes, I was heartbroken for a while, but once again, I picked myself up, dusted myself off and started over.

The divorce was easy, and I haven't seen him for years.

Apparently, they are still together, and I do hope that he is happy now.

GETTING FIT AND HEALTHY

"Fall in love with taking care of yourself. Mind. Body, Spirit." –
Unknown

The next two years were marvellous. I took it easy. I meditated. I got healthy. I switched to pretty much a vegan lifestyle. I worked part-time. Luckily for me, business coaching pays well, so I didn't need to do much of it. I met friends for lunch and coffee. I read. I travelled. To Bali. Greece. To Mexico with the kids.

2012 was a game changer for me. To say that it gave me a different perspective on life has got to be the understatement of the year. It slowed me down for long enough to really think about what I wanted to do with the rest of my life, and as much as I loved coaching, discussing a business owner's profit and loss account or marketing plan was just not going to do it for me anymore.

I wanted to do more of the thing that made my heart sing. I started thinking about what I was doing when I was in my flow – you know, when you are having so much fun that you lose track of time? When you feel energised and alive? I realised that I was in my flow when I was working with young people or adults, helping them to recognise their limiting beliefs. I loved inspiring and empowering people to be the best that they can be. To believe in themselves. I began to understand why we do what we do in ways that I have never understood. I wanted to share that message.

While I was out in Bali, I took part in Wealth Dynamics, which is a profiling system for entrepreneurs. It tells you what kind of entrepreneur you are and what you should be doing to stay in your flow. I discovered that I am a Creator profile which made perfect sense. Creative, head in the clouds, great starter but not always good at finishing! That was me to a tee. I just loved creating stuff. Businesses, websites, programmes. I decided I was going to combine my love of helping people with creating stuff and dedicate my life to creating things that would make a positive difference to people's lives.

Before I had cancer, I was 100 pounds overweight, I ate rubbish more often than not, and I was a workaholic who NEVER exercised. In fact, I could have given you ten good reasons why I couldn't exercise. I knew I had to get in control of my thoughts and work to change my negative beliefs around my ability to lose weight and enjoy exercise or things were never going to change long-term. More importantly, I had to take control of my weight issue once and for all. I started to focus as much on what I was putting in my mind as I was on what I was putting in my mouth.

I set myself a challenge to turn up the volume and listen to what I was saying to myself. The plan was to stop thinking negatively about my weight and my ability to lose it. I started to choose a more helpful way of thinking. There is lots on how to do this is Part Two.

I also recorded myself reciting 20 positive statements or affirmations about healthy eating and exercise, I put a backing track to it and listened to it for hours every day. If I was sat working at my PC, I would have it on quietly in the background. I would listen in my car, when I was cooking dinner, before I went to bed and as soon as I woke up.

Within five days I was going to the gym nearly every day. I couldn't believe it myself. By choosing to think in a more helpful, positive way, over time I have been able to change my belief system about my weight and the ability to lose it and keep it off.

Since then I have gone on to lose nearly 100 pounds (and still losing), I meditate every day, and I now exercise at least 3-5 times a week, and I love it!

My friends and clients could see the results I was getting with my affirmation audio and kept asking me to record one for them. I would send them the list of 400 affirmations, they would choose 20-25, and I would record them with a backing track (usually messing it up on the last one so I would have to start again).

After recording the 29th audio for the fifth time because I'd messed it up, I thought to myself – there has to be an easier way to do this, and so the idea for my first app, *Yes, I Can Do It*, was born.

The Yes, I Can Do It app was the world's first completely personalised motivation and affirmation system (this has now been re-branded HappiMe for Adults). It was a massive learning curve, as I had never developed an app before and didn't have a clue how to start. I found a developer and spent months mapping and flowcharting what I wanted the app to do. It was hugely frustrating but also an empowering and exciting process – one I enjoyed immensely. I was really proud of myself a year later when it was finally available in the app store.

The app was an enormous support during my weight loss journey. I do believe that if I hadn't split my focus equally between my mindset and the food I was eating, I wouldn't have lost the weight and kept it off for over four years.

WHOOPS ROUND 11: DEVASTATING NEWS

"The saddest thing about betrayal is that it never comes from your enemies, it comes from friends and loved ones." – Unknown

I would love to say that Mike's affair was the end of my curveballs, but I can't. On Christmas Day 2015 the bottom dropped out of my world again.

My beautiful daughter Abby had a breakdown on Christmas Day. She was sobbing uncontrollably, and it took a while for me to get it out of her what was wrong. Something she said set big alarm bells clanging in my mind. She said she felt numb inside and had felt that way as long as she could remember. My heart went cold, and I just knew then that something similar had happened to her as had happened to me when I was a child. She eventually disclosed that her stepbrother from my first marriage, who was nine years older, had sexually abused her horrifically for years from a young age. Speaking the words after all this time brought all the emotions to the surface again for her and I thought she was going to break. I just hugged her and wished with all my heart that I could take away her pain.

Hearing that your child has been sexually abused has to be one of the absolute worst things a mother can hear from her child's mouth. I felt like I had been stabbed in the heart. The thought that she had gone through such a horrific time and had kept it to herself for so long was heart-breaking. I think allowing her to understand what had happened to me when I was a child made it easier for her to tell me.

At first, she decided that telling me was enough. She had watched too much courtroom TV to want to put herself through trying to get justice in court. She didn't want to be ripped apart in court and for everyone to know what had happened to her. Like me, Abby had created her "happy persona" and also had struggled with her weight all her life. I wanted her close to me so I could help her heal, so I encouraged her to quit her job and come to work for me. I knew if I could teach her everything that I knew she would have the right tools to get through the coming months. I didn't really have a role for her but just knew it was the right thing to do. As usual, the universe delivered and within weeks I had a new client that paid for Abby's wages every month.

A few weeks later two things happened to change her mind about going to the police.

Firstly, we found out that he had also abused my friend's daughter. The little girl had reported it to the school a few years after it had happened and for their own reason, her parents decided not to tell me. And later that day, we heard that he had a new job as a maintenance person at a holiday camp, so he had access to children. Abby knew deep in her heart that even though the thought of going to the police scared her to death, she had to go in case there was a chance that he was still abusing children.

He was arrested and bailed. Over the next 12 months, the police collected enough evidence to persuade the CPS (Crown Prosecution Service) to take it to court. The fact that the other girl had reported it to her school was a big help as it was on the record. I am very grateful to her for agreeing to stand by Abby and give her statement. Without her, it would have been his word against Abby's, and I am not so sure the CPS would have accepted the case.

It was due to go to court in October 2016, and two days before the court case he walked into the police station and pleaded guilty to a lesser charge. This meant that the girls didn't have to go through the awful ordeal of reliving the experience in a courtroom full of people including their abuser. The lesser sentence meant that he wouldn't spend any time in jail, but Abby was OK with that. She didn't believe that jail would help and she just wanted him on the sex offenders register so he couldn't harm another child. The day we heard that we didn't have to go to court was a very emotional day. Lots of tears and laughter from us and the other girl and her Mum. As we had the following week booked off for court we booked the first flight out of Bristol we could find and spent a few days recuperating in beautiful Greece.

MAKING A DIFFERENCE

"There is nothing more beautiful than someone who goes out of their way to make life beautiful for others." –Mandy Hale

As I mentioned, when I was recovering from my cancer treatment, I was lucky enough to be able to spend a month in Bali on an entrepreneur's retreat. (Another deliberate manifestation – the universe always has my back!) I had the most amazing time. I was there to think about my business and where I wanted to go next with it. I got to spend the month with some amazing people from all over the world. Abby flew out for my third week, and we had a life-changing week together.

During her stay, she had a life-changing session with an amazing and talented coach called Mikal, who helped her discover her passion and her life's purpose. It was an emotional session, and she realised that she wanted to work with children although she wasn't sure how at that point as she didn't want to be a teacher.

While we were out in Bali, I came up with an idea to create a programme to teach children about the power of thinking positively and knew that when the time was right, Abby would join me in it. I just wasn't sure when that would be at that point.

For years, I have said that we need to teach our children the tools and techniques that I was using with my adult clients (which you are going to read about in Part Two of this book). A child with the belief system that I am not good enough will grow into an adult with the same belief system unless something happens to change that. If we can teach our children to get in control of their thoughts at an early age, we can save them years of heartache.

When Abby came to work with me, she started to learn everything you are about to learn. We took those tools and created an amazing coaching programme which Abby uses to work with children with low self-esteem. She works both in schools and privately, and the difference she is making is just fantastic.

I am so very proud of her for finding a bright silver lining in the darkest of all clouds. EFT (Emotional Freedom Therapy), which you will hear lots more about in Part Two, was her saviour. Abby spent months working with Helga, a very beautiful soul and gifted EFT practitioner, who I had also met while out in Bali. Helga helped Abby to release her pain and anguish over what had happened to her, and within four short months, Abby was able to discuss the abuse calmly.

Her abuse could have become her "story" – the story she told herself and others as to why her life wasn't as it should be. It could have been her excuse. Many of the children she works with are vulnerable children, and she has the most incredible connection with them. She gets them, and they get her. The CID officer that worked with her over that 18-month period watched her grow into a very special young woman. She was so impressed with her and the way she handled herself that she suggested that Abby work with the children that she works with. The ones going through the courts right now that don't have much support and just need someone who understands.

There is always a positive if you look hard enough. Sometimes we can't see it at the time, but once we heal we can look back and see that yes, something positive did come out of that awful situation.

For example,

- ✓ The positive from my abuse was that I could help Abby through her abuse.

- ✓ The positive from being bullied and going through domestic violence was personal strength and immense understanding and empathy for others.

- ✓ The positive from having cancer was that it changed my life for the better in so many ways. I am fit and healthy. I am finally in control of my weight for the first time. I am relaxed, and I am doing the thing that makes my heart sing.

- ✓ The positive from losing Mum was that it led our family to EFT. Not only did this life-changing technique help Abby, but it also helped me to finally get rid of my "stuff" and helped my lovely sister Aly through the grief of losing Mum. Myself, Abby and Aly were all so inspired by our experiences with EFT that we trained to be EFT practitioners ourselves.

- ✓ The positive from a cheating husband was that it removed someone from my life that wasn't right for me. Our marriage was already on the rocks, and we were not happy together. Writing about my experiences with the men in my life has been difficult but cathartic. Over the last few months I have revisited some of the most painful moments of my life, and maybe some of you may have been rolling your eyes at my relationships stories, thinking, "For God's sake Jo, what are you playing at!" I know I was as I revisited them. I have learned that I can be happy on my own. I've jumped from one relationship to another for most of my life, and over the last four years, I have come to realise that I don't need a man in my life to make me happy. I can make me happy!

✓ And lastly, the positive to having so much happen in such a short period was that it gave me this story to tell. A story that has hopefully inspired you and helped you to see that when life throws us a curveball, rather than sitting around having a pity party we can pick ourselves up, dust ourselves off and whack that damn ball the hell out of the park!

So, that's enough about me. Let's talk about your happiness.

PART TWO: TOOLS, TIPS, AND TECHNIQUES FOR HAPPINESS

"Happiness is not something you postpone for the future; it is something you design for the present." –Jim Rohn

I'll Be Happy When...

Have you noticed that the western world seems to have adopted a mass "I'll be happy when..." mindset? I'll be happy when... I have lost weight, got a new job, new partner, new car, new business, new house. I'll be happy when.... I get that promotion, have paid all my debts, have more money, am married, divorced or had a baby. I thought like this for most of my adult life. I truly believed that I would be happier when I lost weight. That life would be perfect. That I would suddenly look in the mirror and be wonderfully happy with who I saw looking back at me.

We are often so fixated on what we don't have in our lives that we miss the point. I know I did. I didn't understand that true happiness lies within us, not outside of us. Yes, we can be happy about external events or situations – like a new relationship, a promotion or a pleasurable experience – but that kind of happiness is short-lived. It fades as quickly as our memory of the event fades.

The world is changing. There has been a huge shift in consciousness as millions of people around the world have come to the same conclusion; that there must be a better way to live. That our lives are too busy and too stressful. That we often spend so much time either thinking about the past or worrying about the future that we forget about the present. That this is not a dress rehearsal. That this is our one chance at this life and we must make it count. Life is supposed to be fun, joyful and exciting; not sad, dreary and boring.

"Happiness is a choice, not a destination."

Many of us have read or heard that statement more than once in our lives, but few actually believe it or attempt to put it into practice in their own lives. We nod, agree and say, "that's so true", and carry on in the same way. Allowing other people or situations to determine our happiness (or lack of it in many cases).

Can we really just make up our minds to be happy? The answer is yes. We can. And this book will show you how.

Do you know who the worst culprit is for causing unhappiness? Your chimp brain – the negative voice in your head that chatters away tirelessly. Telling you how rubbish you are, how you are too fat, too young, too old, too shy; not attractive enough, confident enough or clever enough. In the following chapters, you are going to get on a first name basis with your chimp brain. You'll learn how to manage your thinking, and how you can choose a more optimistic and helpful attitude, regardless of what is going on around you. That may seem a tall order right now, but I will teach you all you need to know to quieten that pesky chimp. And when you consistently choose a happier, more optimistic attitude, the universe will move mountains to help you to achieve your dream life. Life is calmer, people are friendlier, and tasks get easier.

So, let's stop with the "I'll be happy when..." crap. Instead, let's learn about the tools, tips, and techniques that will help you to be happier NOW. Today. This minute and the next minute.

The same tools that I have learned and applied over the last 27 years. The same tools that enabled me to stay reasonably sane and happy despite the fact the bottom kept dropping out of my world.

And the same tools that I have used successfully with 100s of coaching clients over the last ten years.

Come on... we're going in!

POSITIVE THINKING VERSUS FEELING MORE OPTIMISTIC

"You will find peace not by trying to escape your problems, but by confronting them courageously. You will find peace not in denial, but in victory." –J. Donald Walters

Positive thinking doesn't work. In fact, it can be dangerous.

Many experts out there that will tell you that if you say something enough times, your subconscious mind will believe it to be true. And that if you stand in front of the mirror, look yourself in the eye and tell yourself that you are the happiest person in the world, you will – if you say it enough times within a short period – become the happiest person in the world. And they will also tell you that if you don't feel happier, it's because you haven't said it enough times, or with enough passion and feeling.

Now, while there is a small element of truth in this, it comes with some massive caveats. If you are already in a fairly good place about your level of happiness, then your chimp brain will be much more likely to accept this kind of positive thinking. If, however, you have been suffering from sadness, grief or depression, simply telling yourself that you are the happiest person in the world is not necessarily going to work. In fact, it may have the opposite effect.

Years ago, one of these "experts" told me that if I looked

myself in the eye every day and told myself, I loved myself enough times, eventually I would believe it. I tried this for months, and it didn't work.

When we try to think positively, and it doesn't work, we feel like a failure, which in turn can make us feel even worse about ourselves. If you are feeling sad or depressed, the last thing you need is someone bouncing in telling you to "just think positively", and all will be happy, wonderful and terrific. You would probably just want to slap them across the face.

Had you bounced in my living room when I was on my "chemo week", to tell me, "just think happy thoughts, and you will feel better", I probably *would have* slapped you across the face. (Well, in my mind I would at least.) I wasn't ready to think positively. I was, however, ready to choose a **slightly more helpful thought**.

This book is not about "positive thinking" – it's about learning to **FEEL more optimistic**. There is a huge difference. It's about choosing a slightly more helpful thought, or a slightly more helpful emotion than you are currently thinking or feeling. Your thoughts, feelings, physical sensations and actions are interconnected, and negative thoughts and feelings can trap you in a vicious cycle. There is a whole chapter on choosing more helpful thoughts later.

Just "thinking positively", is a little like putting a sticking plaster on a gaping wound. It's not going to help. Eventually, whatever problem caused you to feel so awful will start seeping through.

It's a little like standing in the garden saying, "weeds don't grow, weeds don't grow" – they will still grow. Unless you pull them out at the roots or go in with some pretty heavy-duty weed killer. When I discovered EFT a few years ago, within weeks of using it, I understood that it was the heavy-duty weed killer for negative emotions, childhood trauma and self-limiting beliefs. There is a whole chapter on EFT a little later.

This book is not about being in denial. It's not about pretending that we don't have problems. It's not about putting on a brave face and ignoring our "stuff". It's not about denying our feelings and emotions. I did that for the best part of my life and look where it got me.

It's about learning to accept our emotions. It's OK to feel sadness, grief, anger, and frustration. When we acknowledge and accept our problems and emotions, we are able to find a way to move through them much easier. Denying them means that we will never move through them. We'll get stuck.

Rumi, one of the greatest spiritual masters of all time, wrote this beautiful poem that sums it up perfectly:

The Guest House by Rumi

This being human is a guest house.
Every morning a new arrival.
A joy, a depression, a meanness,
some momentary awareness comes
as an unexpected visitor.

Welcome and entertain them all!
Even if they're a crowd of sorrows,
who violently sweep your house
empty of its furniture,
still, treat each guest honourably.
He may be clearing you out

for some new delight.

The dark thought, the shame, the malice,
meet them at the door laughing,
and invite them in.

Be grateful for whoever comes,
because each has been sent
as a guide from beyond.

Simply put, we are the guest house, and it's our job to welcome these emotions, both good and bad. Welcome them into our lives. Accept them. Be grateful for the message they send, and go about your day. Just don't sit with them and have a week-long pity party.

For example:

Jessica's partner had just told her that he wanted to end the relationship. She knew things hadn't been right for a while but was still utterly devastated. She was angry and hurt. She felt betrayed. She felt that her life was over. She felt worthless and unlovable. She spent most of her days thinking about the relationship. What had gone wrong? Was there another woman? Had he ever loved her? The more she thought about it, the worse she felt. She started to get angry. How dare he? She had wasted years of her life on him. It was all she thought about and talked about.

After months of consoling her, friends were starting to lose patience. They told her that it was time to move on. But Jessica was too busy allowing destructive thinking to rule her life. Her negative thoughts were feeding her fear, anger and sense of betrayal. Her bitterness and lack of trust made dating a no-no, and she stayed single for a long time.

Kate's partner had just told her that he wanted to end the relationship. She knew things hadn't been right for a while, but she was still utterly devastated. She was angry and hurt. She felt betrayed. She felt that her life was over. She felt worthless and unlovable. For the first couple of days, she couldn't stop thinking about the relationship. What had gone wrong? Was there another woman? Had he ever loved her?

After a couple of days, she realised that allowing herself to wallow was not going to help. She understood that she needed to accept the situation and move on as best she could. She allowed herself time to grieve over the loss of the relationship but didn't let it dominate her thoughts. She chose to think that she could get over it. She knew one day she wouldn't feel so hurt and chose to believe that maybe there was somebody better out there for her. She acknowledged that she hadn't been happy for a while and that the relationship should have ended sooner. She committed to being more open about her feelings in the next relationship. Within months, she was happy to start dating again.

These two women were in exactly the same situation but had two very different responses which, in turn, led to two very different outcomes.

Emotions and Feelings

"Emotions play out in the theatre of the body. Feelings play out in the theatre of the mind." –Dr. Sarah McKay, Neuroscientist

Although the two words are often used interchangeably, there are distinct differences between feelings and emotions. For starters, they originate in different parts of the brain.

Your **emotions** are primal and instinctive, and stem from our limbic system, which also happens to be where your chimp lives. They have been programmed into our genes over many years of evolution and are hard-wired. Their general purpose is to produce a specific response to a stimulus. For example, you're walking down a dark alley, and realise someone is following you. You instantly go into flight or fight mode. You feel threatened, experience fear (the **emotion**) and feel horror (the **feeling**).

Your **feelings** are sparked by your emotions and coloured by the thoughts, memories, and images that have become subconsciously linked with that particular emotion for you. You have probably seen plenty of scenes on TV where people are attacked after being followed down dark alleys, so your brain has linked this experience with horror. And quite rightly so!

And it can work the other way around too. For example, just thinking about something threatening can trigger an emotional fear response. While individual emotions are temporary, the feelings they evoke often persist and grow over a lifetime.

Because **emotions** cause subconscious **feelings**, which in turn initiate emotions, your life can become a never-ending cycle of painful and confusing emotions and feelings. Negative feelings cause more negative emotions. And around and around it goes.

There is good news: Nothing you can ever experience in life, no matter how terrible, will ever be anything more than a bunch of thoughts, plus a few physical sensations. Can you handle that? I think so.

Although I use the term "negative" or "bad" emotions, in

reality, emotions are neither good or bad. They just are what they are. It's the way we allow those emotions to play out that can be harmful or destructive.

Early Warning Alarm System

Your emotions are part of your early warning alarm system. They are a signal. They are our body and mind's way of telling us when things are going off-track somewhere in our lives. Unfortunately, many of us are very good at ignoring these signals. That's what I did for most of my life. I believed the BS around, "if you think positively enough, everything will be great and you will attract the life of your dreams".

We must learn to acknowledge and accept our emotions – only then can we find a way through them.

There Are Only Two Key Emotions – Fear and Love

All human actions are motivated at their deepest level by two key emotions: fear or love. You can only choose one at a time. All other emotions and feelings are based within one or the other. All positive emotions such as joy, happiness, contentment and peace flow from love; and all negative emotions such as annoyance, anger, hate, jealousy and anxiety flow from fear. We cannot feel these two emotions at the same time, so if we are in a place of love, we are not in a place of fear, and when we are in a place of fear, we can't be in a place of love.

The closer you can come to identifying your emotions as love or fear, the closer you are to determining which emotion is driving you. You will find that fear affects your whole life and is the cause of most your problems.

After reading the above paragraph, Kate, my wonderful

editor made the following statement:

"Just a thought here. I think love can also be damaging if we spend all of our energy making other people happy, rather than looking after ourselves. Also, can't love lead to problems, e.g. with food and weight? If you show your love through feeding, this can damage the ones on the receiving end of your food."

I thought this was an excellent point and definitely worth exploring further.

Spending all our energy trying to make others happy is very common. Especially in women and particularly in mothers. In my experience, this nearly always stems from a basis of fear. Whether that is a fear of rejection, fear of failure, fear of confrontation or the most common is the good old "I'm not good enough" fear.

Let me give you an example...

Bridie is a 40-year-old mother of three grown-up boys, who are all still living at home. She works part-time in her own business and sometimes struggles to keep the plates spinning. She loves her family and wants them to be happy and healthy. She gets up early to make sure the house is clean and tidy. She spends hours planning and cooking healthy meals for them every day. She cooks, she cleans, she washes and irons. She tries to keep the peace between the four grown men in her house and spends her weekends doing whatever the family wants to do. She is exhausted. There's just is no time for her. She is so busy making sure everyone else is happy that she has no time for herself.

Bridie thinks everything must be perfect for her family to be happy. She fears letting her family down. She is scared of what her husband will say if dinner is not on the table at the right time. Or what her friends will think if the house is a mess. She thinks she must be the perfect mum and wife. She thinks her sole job is to make her family happy. Although Bridie may think her actions are born out of love for her family, in reality, they are based in fear.

Sam *is a 40-year-old mother of three grown-up boys, who are all still living at home. She works part-time in her own business and sometimes struggles to keep the plates spinning. She loves her family and wants them to be happy and healthy. She didn't seem to have time for herself anymore. She likes to read and meditate, visit friends or watch a movie but there always seemed to be more important things to do. She commits to find some "me time" in her day.*

She starts to think about ways she could free up time. Perhaps she could do her shopping online rather than struggling to get to the supermarket? Or she could send her husband or one of the boys with a list? She explained to her family that she wasn't happy and asked for their help. She asked them to help out around the house more. She drew up a simple chores list. Perhaps they could each be responsible for dinner one day a week? They each agreed to pay an extra £6 housekeeping every week, so she could get a cleaner to come in for a couple of hours. Gradually she managed to claw back some precious "me time".

Sam understands that her happiness is as important as her family's happiness. She deserves to have some quality me time. Her decisions are made from a basis of love for herself.

Kate's second example about love and comfort leading to problems with food and weight is also worth considering.

Many of us associate food with treats, awards, celebrations, and happiness. Those of us that eat for comfort do so because for the short time we are eating, we feel happier. The food fulfils a need in us that is not being met elsewhere. Whether that need is loneliness, boredom or anxiety – they are all based in fear.

Get into the habit of checking in with your emotions and ask yourself whether you are coming from a place of love or fear.

For example, I am "nearly vegan" – which is a great phrase I read on Facebook recently. At the end of December 2014, someone challenged me to Veganuary (which I can't ever manage to say without making it sound rather rude!). It basically means you eat a vegan diet for the whole of January.

So – no dairy, fish, meat or animal products of any kind. For 31 days. I had been studying the research behind dairy and meat products in relation to cancer, so I thought, "why not?". I didn't eat a huge amount of meat anyway. Not only was it one of the easiest things I had ever done, but I felt great. I had an endless supply of energy, and I never felt bloated, so I decided to stay with it since then.

I eat out a lot, so I occasionally have dairy and the odd piece of fish, especially if I am on holiday, but I am mainly a vegan. That decision was based out of love for myself – I felt awesome and wanted to carry on feeling that way. The fact that I felt that it was hugely beneficial for my body was a super added benefit.

I have a friend that has also gone through cancer and is desperately trying to be a vegan at the moment. She constantly worries that if she eats meat, dairy or sugar, her cancer will come back. She is coming from a place of fear.

Once we notice that we are in fear, we can choose to act out of love instead. To decide to trust that things will work out, to be compassionate and open, and to feel connected to others and the world.

How do we step out of fear and anxiety into love and joy?

First, treat yourself with self-compassion. Instead of judging and criticising yourself, talk as if you were speaking to your best friend. Your best friend has your back, supports you, encourages you, consoles you, and celebrates with you.

Make a commitment to only speak to yourself in the same way that you would speak to your best friend. Would you tell your best friend that she was fat, boring, not good enough or stupid? Would you tell her that she was a loser who always messed up? Would you tell her that no one liked her or that everyone thought she was an idiot? Of course you wouldn't. But if you are like most people that I have worked with, you will be saying things like that to yourself every single day.

Your Decision-Making process

As with many issues, the first step to improvement is awareness. Look back at the important decisions you've made and ask yourself if they were made from a basis of fear or love.

Here are some of mine to get you thinking:

- I chose to be a chef out of fear – I didn't know what else to do, and I was worried I wouldn't have a job.

- I married my first husband out of fear – I was worried that I wouldn't find someone else that would take on a single mother.

- I left him out of fear – I was worried that I would spend the rest of my life unhappy.

- I yo-yo dieted for years out of fear – I was worried about what I looked like and what others would think about me.

- I lost weight for the last time out of love – for myself and my children.

- I cleared my "stuff" out of love – I wanted to feel at peace with myself.

- I meditate and practise daily "feel good" rituals like gratitude, affirmations and visualising, out of love for myself – not only do these daily rituals help me to feel fantastic, they also allow wonderful abundance to flow into my life.

It wasn't until I understood this concept that I began to make decisions from a basis of love. So don't be surprised if the most important decisions you made in the past were made from a basis of fear.

Sometimes it's as simple as looking at it from a different perspective.

For example:

Louise wants to change her job because she doesn't get on with her manager. She hates going to work so she can't wait to leave. She moans about her manager daily and is applying for every job she sees. She's stressed and desperate to get out. She doesn't care what job she gets, as long as it's better than this one. She is coming from a place of fear.

***Alison** works for the same manager and also wants to leave. She's not been happy for a while and knows she deserves to be treated better. She understands that her manager is not a bad person – she's just not a very good manager. She recognises that allowing herself to get upset every day isn't going to make her manager a better manager, so she decides not to allow the situation to get her down while she looks for a new job. She knows the situation is only temporary. She starts to think about what kind of job she would enjoy. She thinks about the kind of company she would like to work for. She takes an online career quiz and researches what kind of role would utilise her skills best. She's excited that she is moving forward in her quest for a more fulfilling career. She is coming from a place of love.*

Chapter in a nutshell

- Learn to FEEL more optimistically, don't just THINK more positively.
- Get your head out of the sand. Learn to acknowledge and accept your problems and emotions so you can move through them.
- All your decisions and actions are rooted in love or fear.

Actions

- Start choosing a slightly more helpful thought or emotion. When you feel a little better, choose another even more helpful thought or emotion. Take baby steps. Lots more on this in the next two chapters.
- Check in with yourself a few times each day and ask yourself what emotion you are feeling. Are you angry, sad and anxious? Or calm, peaceful and happy? Note the emotion and where you feel it in your body. What message is the emotion sending you? What needs to change? What do you need to do differently? What are you ignoring or not tending too? Start taking small steps to improve what needs to be improved or to change what needs to be changed.
- Think about the major decisions you have made in your life. Were they based on fear or love? Before you make any decisions in the future, consider how you can make them from a basis of love. Download the template at www.jorichings.com/whoops
- Be gentle and compassionate with yourself. Treat yourself as if you are the most important person in your life. Because you are.

A LITTLE LESSON ON HOW THE BRAIN WORKS

"Change your thoughts, and you change your world." –Norman Vincent Peale

Meet your Chimp

Your chimp lives in your limbic system, the emotional part of your brain in charge of survival. His number one job is to keep you safe, so he doesn't like change. Your chimp likes you to stay in your comfort zone, as that's where he feels safe. Whenever he feels that you are about to step out of your comfort zone, he will do everything in his power to stop you. Filling your head with worries, making you feel physically ill and turning you into a master procrastinator; these are just a few of his sneaky techniques.

Your chimp resides in the limbic "primal" part of your brain. Your chimp is the part of your brain that worries, gets mad or upset. The part of your brain that tells you that you are stupid, likely to fail or that nobody likes you. Whenever you feel like you are not good enough or worry about what other people are thinking about you – your chimp is in control. Your chimp can be male or female, old or young. It's entirely up to you – it's your chimp.

In his life-changing book, *The Chimp Paradox*, Dr. Steve Peters suggests that you give your chimp a name. This helps you to disassociate from his or her negative chatter, so you can recognise when he or she is in control. Mine is called Charlie.

I imagine Charlie's voice as a well-intentioned child. He means well but doesn't really know what's good for me anymore.

Meet your HappiTar

Your HappiTar – your Happiness Avatar – is the part of your brain that cheers you on – the sensible, logical, more evolved, pre-frontal cortex part of your brain. This is the part of your brain that says things like...

- Let's start healthy eating.

- No, we don't need another glass of wine.

- Yes, we should get up and go the gym now.

- Let's get up as soon as the alarm goes off tomorrow.

- We are good enough.

- People do like us.

- We can do it.

Unfortunately, most of us don't listen to this part of our brain very much.

Your Subconscious Mind and Your Computer

Your subconscious mind is like a massive computer with a gigantic memory bank. Its capacity is virtually limitless. It permanently stores everything that ever happens to you.

By the time you reach the age of 21, you've probably stored more than one hundred times the contents of the entire Wikipedia site!

Your subconscious mind is subjective. It does not think or reason independently; it merely obeys the commands it receives from your conscious mind.

Your conscious mind commands and your subconscious mind obeys.

An important fact to understand about your subconscious mind is that it is listening intently to everything you say. Every second, of every minute, of every hour, of every day; it is monitoring what you say to yourself. Especially what you say about yourself when you are by yourself.

It takes the words that you use, and the pictures that you create in your conscious mind, and uses them to create your beliefs and ways of being. These beliefs then become "programmes" that run you, just like the programmes that run your computer.

If you constantly tell yourself that you are no good at maths, public speaking, cooking or dancing – you will never be any good at maths, public speaking, cooking or dancing. Your brain will find a way to make you mess up! That's what it does.

For example:

- If you feel angry when someone laughs at you – you are running the angry programme.

- If you get anxious before public speaking or social event – you are running the anxious programme.

- If you are annoyed because someone was rude to you – you are running the annoyed programme.

What you think about, you bring about.

People with poor time management skills are an excellent example of how a belief can run our lives. Over the years, I have coached many clients who were lousy at time management, as is often the case with small business owners. They rush around telling themselves that there aren't enough hours in the day, that they can't get on top of things however hard they try, and that something always gets in the way of them being able to plan their day properly. And it's never their fault, of course.

I learned the hard way that I could teach them every time management tip, tool, and technique in the book, but unless they were willing to work on the belief that caused the problem (i.e. "I am rubbish at time management"), then they would always end up back where they started. Always. Your subconscious can only do what you tell it to do. You command. It obeys.

This is the exact same reason why 98% of people who lose weight, will regain it again. 98%. No wonder the weight loss industry is such a lucrative industry. Dieters change their behaviour in the short term (i.e. eat more veggies, avoid sugar, exercise more) but they don't change their programming. The belief that made them overweight in the first place – I am an overweight person.

And this is also why a similar % of people that win the lottery will be broke again within five years. They will end up with roughly the same in the bank as before they won. Again, they change their behaviour short term but don't change their belief system. Their identity stays the same – "I am a poor person".

You are where you are right now because of your thoughts and beliefs. You created you. This may be a sobering thought for some.

Another way to think about this is to imagine that your conscious mind – the one you talk to yourself with – is like a camera and your subconscious mind is like the darkroom where your pictures are developed. When you talk to yourself either positively or negatively, your camera – your conscious mind – is constantly taking pictures and sending them to the darkroom – your subconscious mind – to be developed.

Imagine taking lots of pictures of an overweight person. When you look at them you wouldn't expect to see pictures of a slim person, would you? Same rules apply. What goes in, must come out!

A couple of really important facts here. Firstly, your subconscious mind doesn't know if you are kidding or serious. It doesn't know when you put yourself down in jest. It doesn't know when you are being flippant.

Secondly, it doesn't know the difference between a good belief and a harmful one. It will just create your reality based on what you say to yourself. Its job is to prove that what you say is right. It wants you to be right.

Have you noticed that people who say...

- I can't say no – can't say no?

- I am always late – are always late?

- I am unorganised – are unorganised?

- I am impatient – don't have any patience?

- I am rubbish at maths – are no good at maths?

- I never lose weight – never lose weight?

- I am not very confident – are not very confident?

Get the picture?

Just like you can change the programmes on a computer, you can also change the beliefs, programmes and habits in your brain.

You can choose whether you listen to your chimp or your HappiTar and, more importantly, you can learn to recognise when your chimp is running the show.

Fight or Flight

Your chimp brain receives information much quicker than your HappiTar. Your chimp is constantly on guard, and as soon as he senses danger, he dashes to your computer to find out what programme to run. He will grab the worry programme, the angry programme, the eat too much or drink too much programme or whatever programme you currently use in that kind of situation. He's scared. He's in fight or flight mode.

Fight or flight is the emotional response to our body's primitive, automatic, inborn response that prepares the body to fight or flee from the perceived attack, harm or threat to our survival.

When we experience too much stress, whether from internal worry or external circumstances, chemicals like adrenaline, noradrenaline and cortisol are released into our bloodstream, which causes our body to undergo a series of very dramatic changes.

Our respiratory rate increases. Blood is shunted away from our digestive system and directed into our muscles and limbs. Our pupils dilate. Our awareness intensifies. Our eyesight sharpens. Our impulses quicken. Our perception of pain diminishes. Our immune system mobilises with increased activation.

We become prepared — physically and psychologically — for fight or flight. We scan and search our environment, "looking for the enemy".

This crucial response to danger is important and is one of the key reasons the human race is still alive and hasn't been eaten by tigers. Unfortunately, your chimp doesn't understand the difference between a real tiger and a paper tiger. The same neurons will fire in your brain when you are stressed or worried about a meeting with your boss as those that fire when you are being chased by an actual tiger. Your body will feel the same dramatic changes. Your chimp will do everything in its power to stop you getting "eaten by a tiger". He will get into your head with the "what ifs", he will make your heart pound, your hands shake and your stomach churn.

Understand that your chimp means well but doesn't really know what is good for you. Back in the caveman days, flight or fight was crucial. Nowadays, not so much. We are very unlikely to get chased by a tiger, so we need to train our chimp to recognise the difference between a real tiger and a paper one.

We are going to develop new, positive, more helpful programmes; so next time your chimp goes looking for what programme to run, he can choose the "walk away" programme, "take a deep breath" programme or "I can do this" programme. We are going to rewire your brain!

Neuroplasticity: *The brain's ability to reorganise itself by forming new neural connections throughout life. Neuroplasticity allows the neurons (nerve cells) in the brain to adjust their activities in response to new situations or changes in their environment.*

A thought is just a thought.

Just because we think something, it doesn't necessarily mean it's true. What gives a thought power is the feeling we attach to it and how much we focus on it. Thinking about things we can't control or worrying about things that may never happen is utterly pointless. All it does is make us feel bad.

We can just as easily learn to recognise what we are doing and make a choice to think a more helpful thought. One that doesn't make us feel rubbish about ourselves!

But what if what you are thinking is true?

Sometimes we worry about things that are true. They are not paper tigers but the real scary stuff, like life-threatening diseases. We can't always control what is going on around us, other people and situations, but we can control the way we react to it. More on how to do that later.

Every time you choose to think or act differently, you are strengthening your new "programmes". There is always a choice. Choosing to approach life, events and situations with a more helpful attitude leads to more helpful, positive thoughts, more optimistic feelings and better actions and behaviours.

Left to its own devices, your chimp will have you believing that the worse will happen and the sky will actually fall down.

Experts estimate that we have somewhere between 30,000-60,000 thought processes per day and that 80% of them are either negative, self-sabotaging or neutral (as in "what's for dinner" or "I need to pick up the dry cleaning").

I actually think it is much higher than 80%. How much time have you spent over the last week thinking how proud you are of yourself or how great you are? I can pretty much guarantee it won't have been 20% of your time. We spend most of the day either ruminating over yesterday or worrying about tomorrow.

So, even if we take the lower figure of 30,000 and estimate that only 50% of what we say is negative – and that's being conservative – then the average person still has over 5 million negative thoughts a year. Is it any wonder many people go through life feeling unhappy, unfulfilled and fed up?

From A Thought to a Belief.

What is a belief?

A belief is anything that you believe to be true.

Is it necessarily true?

No, it's not. It's just what you believe to be true at a particular point in your life, based on the best available evidence you have at that time. There is no such thing as a true belief or false belief. There are only useful ones that help and support us or harmful ones that sabotage us and stop us from achieving happiness and success.

So, can a belief be changed?

Yes, definitely it can. Sometimes it can be relatively easy to change a belief.

Let's take Father Christmas as an example. At one point in your life, you happily believed in Father Christmas. Then someone, usually a well-meaning older brother or sister, told you that he wasn't real. When you first heard the upsetting news, your evidence that Father Christmas was real started to change. You were no longer convinced. Perhaps you asked your parents or friends if this was, in fact, true. When the story was confirmed, you formed a new belief that was based on the new best available evidence.

Another example is when someone is happily married, and they find out that their husband or wife is having an affair. In the blink of an eye, the belief that you have a happy marriage is shattered.

These are two pretty extreme examples. Is it usually that easy? No. Not always. It will depend on how deep the belief is. Some of your beliefs will be extremely deep-rooted, so you may need a little help from EFT (aka the heavy duty weed killer) to shift them. But you CAN change many of your beliefs easily enough, as long as you are prepared to put in a little bit of effort.

So, let's talk about how a belief is formed.

A belief starts as a thought. Either we notice something about ourselves, we say something to ourselves, or we hear someone else say something about us. The seed of a belief has been planted (usually by a well-meaning chimp). A neural pathway has been created in your brain.

Your subconscious mind will then work tirelessly to make your thoughts come true. It will take note of the negative thoughts and file them neatly under "Things We Believe to be True About Ourselves", and make sure you don't forget them. The neural pathway will get deeper and deeper, a little like a groove on a record. A belief will be formed, which will create a habitual way of thinking or doing – a programme. One which will stay with you until you replace it with a more helpful programme.

All habitual ways of thinking and doing start the same way. The more you repeat your negative self-talk, the deeper your negative beliefs will go. The deeper the negative beliefs go, the more likely you are to say the negative belief. Eventually, it becomes a self-fulfilling prophecy. You say it, your subconscious mind believes it and helps you become it. You command. It obeys. And around and around it goes! Your thoughts determine your actions.

Imagine you installed Windows 10 on your laptop or computer. It's not going to start running Windows 8, however much willpower you have, or however much you want it to. You'll need to install a different programme. Same goes for your brain. If you want more beneficial habits and behaviours, you need to install new ways of thinking first.

What you think about, you bring about.

Just in case you didn't get the message, I really want to drive this point home as I believe it is one of the most important things that you will ever learn.

I will say it again...

What you think about, you bring about!

Don't take my word for it, here's just a sample of the thousands of quotes from famous people on the subject...

Buddha

"All that we are is a result of what we have thought."

Winston Churchill

"You create your own universe as you go along."

Gandhi

"A man is but the product of his thoughts. What he thinks he becomes."

W. Clement Stone

"Whatever the mind can conceive, it can achieve."

Henry Ford

"Whether you think you can or you think you can't, either way, you are right."

Shakespeare

"Nothing is unless our thinking makes it so."

Jack Canfield

"Whatever you focus on, think about, read about, and talk about intensely, you're going to attract more of into your life."

Napoleon Hill

"The vast majority of people are born, grow up, struggle, and

go through life in misery and failure, not realising that it would be just as easy to switch over and get exactly what they want out of life, not recognising that the mind attracts the thing it dwells upon."

Hopefully, you got the message there. Your thoughts and beliefs are holding you back. You're not a failure. Change your thoughts and beliefs, and you will crack your problems forever. How wonderful is that?

And therefore, you will only make long-term changes in your life if you work on your beliefs and self-talk first. If you want to change your life – you must start by changing your beliefs.

Chapter in a nutshell

- Your chimp is the emotional part of your brain. Your chimp is responsible for your negative self-talk. He gets all information first.

- Your HappiTar is the sensible, logical part of your brain.

- Your computer is where your automatic programmes and beliefs are stored.

- Your conscious mind commands. Your subconscious mind obeys.

- A belief starts as a thought. What you think about, you bring about.

- Creating new behaviours starts with new thinking habits.

Actions

- Name your chimp and start to recognise when he or she is in control.

- Read *The Chimp Paradox* by Dr Steve Peters.

*The Chimp is based on The Chimp Model, a fascinating concept from a superb book called *The Chimp Paradox*, by Dr. Steve Peters. We have used a simple, adapted version for use in the HappiMe app, as I felt it was such a simple concept for children to understand. I have recommended his book to hundreds of people over the last few years. Highly recommended to you too!

TAKE RESPONSIBILITY

"There are only two options regarding commitment; you're either in, or you're out. There's no such thing as life in-between." –Pat Riley

This chapter is about taking total responsibility for yourself right now. For your health, your weight, your relationships, your career and your life choices. This is not about blaming yourself or beating yourself up. It's simply about accepting that, for the most part, you are where you are because of your thoughts and actions.

Many years of coaching have taught me that people who do not take responsibility for their lives are unlikely to succeed in making significant changes. This book will be a great help, but it is you who must take responsibility for you. You are in control of your attitude, your thoughts and your actions. And you always have been, but maybe you just didn't realise it.

"Be careful of your thoughts, for your thoughts become your words.
Be careful of your words, for your words become your actions.
Be careful of your actions, for your actions become your habits.
Be careful of your habits, for your habits become your character.
Be careful of your character, for your character becomes your destiny."
–Author unknown

You always have the power to change how you feel about any

aspect of your life. You may not be able to change the situation, but you can change the way you feel about it.

It's only when you acknowledge and accept that everything you are, or will ever be, is up to you. That you can eliminate the excuse making that can so often prevent you from succeeding.

When you first recognise this fact, it can seem like a huge responsibility. Why is it all up to little ole me? When you accept that you are responsible for every action you take and every decision you make, you come to understand that there is virtually nothing that you can't achieve. How empowering is that?

Is Your Glass Half Full or Half Empty?

"We don't have to just think whatever stinkin' thinkin' falls into our heads." –Joyce Meyers

The standard "glass-half-full or half-empty" saying is often used to emphasize the difference between positive and negative thinking, or optimism and pessimism. The expression is so well known that people and personality types are often referred to as "glass-half-full" or "glass-half-empty".

Personally, I don't think what is in your glass is anywhere near as important as how you feel about what's in your glass. If you look at the half empty part of your glass and fret, worry or get angry about what's missing – you will never be happy. And if you look at the half-full part of the glass and get cross or upset at what's in there – you will never be happy either.

It's not what we have or haven't got that's important. What's important is how we feel about what we have or haven't got.

We all know people that have nothing but are still happy. And we all know people that seem to have everything but are still unhappy.

What many people forget is that we can choose our attitude every single minute, of every single hour, of every single day. There is always a choice. Every time something happens to us in life, we can choose to react positively, learn the lessons that need to be learned, take responsibility and move on. Or we can choose to behave in a negative way, where we blame other people or situations and make endless excuses.

We can choose to wake up and tell ourselves that today is going to be a great day or not.

It's a choice.

We can choose to allow ourselves to wallow in self-pity for a week because something went wrong... **or not.**

We can choose to give ourselves a hard time because we messed up at work... **or not.**

We can choose to blame our partner for our relationship not working... **or not.**

We can choose to make excuses like I'm too old, too young, not confident enough, not pretty enough, not clever enough... or **not.**

We always have the power to choose more helpful, more positive thoughts. We have the power to turn our attention wherever we like.

Unfortunately, we often forget this and give our power away. We let other people or situations control our happiness. We let our chimp take control when things don't go our way. We sulk, get upset, throw our toys out of our pram, stomp about, huff and puff, swear, have a pity party, go into a bubble or whatever is your chimp's way of behaving when things don't go your way. What a complete and utter waste of time and energy. It rarely, if ever, does any good.

Quite often we cannot control the things that are happening around us, but we CAN control the attitude with which we choose to react. A situation or person cannot "make" us feel annoyed, upset, stressed or fed up. True – people can do things or say things to us that could evoke these emotions, but we still choose to allow the emotion to happen. We are in control of ourselves, nobody else.

When something bad happens to us, it doesn't have to ruin our day or our lives. We can choose a different reaction. We can learn to pick ourselves up, dust ourselves off and go at it again.

Allowing yourself to worry is a habit. It's just a skill you have developed like cleaning your teeth but with none of the benefits.

Allowing yourself to feel anger or rage towards another person is a little like picking up a burning coal to throw – you are the one who will get burnt.

Refusing to forgive someone is a little like swallowing poison and hoping the other person will get sick. You are the one who suffers most.

You can learn to recognise when your chimp is running the show. You can learn to choose a more helpful way of thinking. You can learn to choose a better attitude.

Jack Canfield, the author of *The Success Principles*, puts it like this...

E + R = O (Event + Response = Outcome)

The only thing we are in control of in that equation is our response. The event (situation, conversation, etc.) is what it is. An event. What makes it painful or upsetting is our thinking about the event. If we want a different outcome, we need to choose a different response.

The event is the event. The situation is the situation. What he or she did, or said, is what it is.

We can't change that. It is what it is, so stop worrying, moaning or fretting about things you can't change. Learn to choose a more helpful response. One that doesn't involve you having a pity party, throwing your toys out of your pram or heading for the biscuit tin!

"There is nothing either good or bad but thinking makes it so".
–William Shakespeare

An extreme example of this can be found in one of the most inspirational books ever written, a book called *Man's Search for Meaning* by Viktor Frankl. Frankl, an Austrian neurologist and psychiatrist, chronicles the experiences he endured as a concentration camp inmate in Auschwitz during the Second World War. His experiences led him to discover the importance of finding meaning in all forms of existence, even the most brutal ones, and thus, a reason to continue living.

"Between stimulus and response, there is a space. In that space is our power to choose our response. In our response lies our growth and our freedom. Everything can be taken away from a

man but one thing: the last of the human freedom – to choose one's attitude in any given set of circumstances, to choose one's own way."

I passionately believe that you can learn to master your thinking and therefore your emotions, but you must first acknowledge that you are capable of doing so. Most of us have been taught that we are not in control of our emotions, so we say things like, "you made me so angry", as opposed to "I choose to be angry because you said that". It's a minor but very important distinction. Understanding that no one can force you to feel a fear-based emotion is hugely empowering.

Yes, your partner, your family, your friends, your colleagues or your boss can all do all kinds of things that have the potential to make you angry, sad, fed-up or anxious, but the choice to feel these emotions is your responsibility.

I was talking to an old client this morning, and he reminded me of a conversation we had many years ago regarding this. He said: "I can remember moaning to you about how a situation around a certain person was making me unhappy, and you said something profound that has really changed the way I look at life. You said, 'so are you telling me that you are letting other people take control of your happiness?' The more I thought about it, the more I understood what you were saying. Put like that it sounded pretty silly. Of course, I am not going to put my happiness in the hands of another person. I decided to stop handing the responsibility of my happiness over to others. It was life-changing."

There is always a choice.

Positive thinkers

- Take complete responsibility for their lives.

- Do not allow themselves to make excuses.

- Don't blame other people, events or situations.

- Do not waste time blaming themselves either.

- Understand that they don't have to be perfect.

- Accept that life goes a little off course at times.

- Understand that they are in control of themselves. They are not victims.

Negative thinkers...

- Blame everyone or everything else.

- Are in denial.

- Will procrastinate.

- Make excuses.

Which are you?

Chapter in a nutshell

- Take responsibility for where you are in life and how you feel about it.

- Understand that you have the power to change how you feel about any aspect of your life.

- Choose your attitude daily.

- Choose your thoughts carefully.

- Remember, Event + Response = Outcome. You are in control of your response. Always. Don't give your power away.

Actions

- Recognise your excuses. Download the template at www.jorichings.com/whoops. List them down, so you are aware of them. Understand that excuses are often your chimp's way of making you procrastinate. You now know better! Don't let him win.

- Understand what "story" you have been telling yourself and others as to why you can't change or improve.

- Understand where you are giving your power away. Who are you handing responsibility for your happiness to?

- Make a conscious decision daily to choose a more helpful way of thinking and feeling. Be alert to chimp talk!

A LITTLE COGNITIVE
BEHAVIOURAL THERAPY (CBT)

"Good morning is not a greeting; it's a decision." –Anonymous

CBT is another simple but very powerful tool for your emotional resilience toolbox. It helps you to recognise that your thoughts, feelings, physical sensations and actions are all interconnected. Simply put, CBT combines cognitive therapy (examining the things you think) and behaviour therapy (examining the things you do).

As you may well know, negative thoughts and feelings can often trap you in a vicious cycle.

Just like E+R=O (event + response = outcome), CBT emphasises that it is not the situation that causes the emotional distress, it's our interpretation of the event or situation which causes the anxiety, worry or anger. It works by recognising our negative thought patterns and encourages us to challenge them, as well as learning how to change unhelpful behaviours such as avoidance.

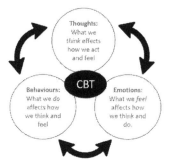

Sue *has a chance of a promotion. Part of her new role will involve public speaking, something that terrifies her. Her thoughts, emotions, physical symptoms and behaviours are all influenced by each other. She thinks that she will make a fool of herself and that everyone will think she's stupid. Her heart beats faster, and she has a cold sweat just thinking about it. Because of this, she doesn't go for the promotion. She uses the excuse that it will be too much pressure and that she is happy where she is. Knowing that these are just excuses causes Sue to feel even more anxious and embarrassed, and strengthens her negative thoughts about herself.*

Jan *has a chance of a promotion. Part of her new role will involve public speaking, something that terrifies her. Her thoughts, emotions, physical symptoms and behaviours are all influenced by each other. She thinks that she will make a fool of herself and that everyone will think she's stupid. Her heart beats faster, and she has a cold sweat just thinking about it. Because she really wants the promotion, she knows she must find a way to overcome this. She researches courses on public speaking and finds the perfect course at her local college. She explores hypnotherapy and EFT as ways of handling her nerves. She looks for opportunities to speak up. She starts to be more vocal in team meetings. Every time she does this, her confidence grows. She goes for the promotion, knowing that if other people can overcome their fear of public speaking, then so can she. She feels good about herself. She is proud of herself for getting outside her comfort zone.*

Jan used a CBT model called Graded Exposure. Rather than jumping in with her first public speaking engagement and frightening the living daylights out of herself, she gradually increased her exposure to her fear, by speaking up in team meetings. Baby steps. That's all we need to take.

ANTs

When we are feeling low or anxious, it is common to have automatic negative thoughts (ANTs). These unhelpful thoughts pop into our minds without any effort.

Thought Traps

When catching your ANTs, you may also find that there is a theme to your negative thinking. In CBT, these thought distortions are called Thought Traps.

Have a look at the following list and see if you can recognise any of your thinking patterns. (You can download these and a template for recognising your own ANTs at www.jorichings.com/whoops.)

All or nothing thinking:

You see things in extreme or in black and white.

Example: *If you get 76% on a test, you feel like a failure because you didn't get a perfect score.*

Example 2: *You are on a healthy eating plan, and someone brings a cake to work. After eating a piece, you think, "I've completely blown my diet now" and so proceed to eat a bar of chocolate, two packets of crisps and a bowl of ice cream.*

Mental filter:

You pick out a single negative detail and dwell on it, viewing the whole situation as negative. You refuse to notice any positives or anything that went well/you did well.

Example 1: *You are cooking lunch and overcooked the broccoli. You think to yourself, "what an idiot. Everyone must*

135

think I am a rubbish cook".

Example 2: *You run a project meeting at work which is complimented and praised by 95% percent of the team – but you dwell and focus on the 5% of feedback that you could have done a slightly better job. This leaves you convinced you didn't do well enough and not only don't you recognise and enjoy the praise being offered but you decide not to participate in future events.*

Emotional reasoning:

You assume that your negative emotions reflect the way things really are, i.e. "I feel like a failure; therefore, I am one".

Example 1: *Even though your partner hasn't shown you any evidence to suspect that he or she has been unfaithful, you think, "I know they are unfaithful because I feel jealous".*

Other examples:

"I feel guilty; therefore, I must have done something bad";

"I feel overwhelmed and hopeless; therefore, my problems must be impossible to solve";

"I feel inadequate; therefore, I must be a worthless person";

"I'm not in the mood to do anything; therefore, I might as well just lie in bed";

"I'm furious with you; this proves that you've been acting badly and trying to take advantage of me".

Disqualifying the positive:

Whenever you have a negative experience, you dwell on it

and conclude, "That proves what I've known all along – I'm not good enough". In contrast, when you have a positive experience, you tell yourself, "That was a fluke. It doesn't count".

Example 1: *A friend compliments you on a dinner you made, but you decide that "they are just saying that to be nice" or "they are trying to get something out of me".*

Example 2: *You are at a party, and someone ignores you. You will not only remember the person who ignored you, but you will also forget or downplay the others that chatted to you for hours, saying, "oh they just felt sorry for me".*

Example 3: *"I've only cut back from smoking 40 cigarettes a day to 10. It doesn't count because I've not fully given up yet."*

Should/must/ought statements:

You set yourself standards of what you perceive you and others "should" or "must" be doing. These standards are often too high and unrealistic. "Should statements" can be directed against yourself causing guilt, or they can be directed at other people causing anger and frustration.

Example 1*: You don't like going out with a particular friend but feel as though you should, because you have known her for years*

Example 2: *You are in a bad mood because of something your boss said. You feel that your partner should be more understanding. "They ought to have been more considerate of my feelings. They should know that would upset me."*

Over-generalisation:

You see a single negative event as proof that other similar events will turn out the same way.

Example 1: *If you fail to get a job you interview for, you decide you are never going to get a job.*

Example 2: *You might go on one unsuccessful date and decide you are never going to find a partner.*

Personalisation:

You automatically assume responsibility and blame for negative events that are not under your control.

Example: *You feel it's all your fault that your son injured his leg even though you weren't at home when it happened. He was safe with a relative, but your thoughts were, "if only I didn't go out – if I stayed home it wouldn't have happened, it's my fault".*

Example 2: *"If she hadn't yelled at me, I wouldn't have been angry and wouldn't have had that car accident."*

How many of these thought traps have you fallen into? As with most things, just being aware of what you are doing will help you to choose a more helpful way of thinking.

Jumping to conclusions:

You come to a negative conclusion even though there are no definite facts that support this conclusion.

Mind reading – you conclude that someone is reacting negatively to you, but you do not check this out with them.

Example 1: *You are at a party, and people are whispering. You don't like what you are wearing, so you decide, "everyone is laughing at me".*

Fortune telling – you anticipate that things will turn out badly, and you feel that your prediction is an already established fact.

Example 2: *You are going to take your driving test and "know" that you are going to fail.*

Catastrophising:

You expect disaster to strike and that the disaster will be of massive proportions. You tell yourself that something terrible will happen and you won't be able to handle it.

Example 1: *You send out the wrong letter to a client at work, and this turns into, "I will now lose my job, and then I won't be able to pay my bills, and then I will lose my house".*

Example 2: *You fail your driving test. This leads to, "I'll never pass my test" and, "I'll never be able to drive" and, "I won't get a good job if I can't drive".*

Labelling

This is over-generalising at its worst. Instead of describing your error, you attach a negative label to yourself: "I'm stupid."

When someone else's behaviour bothers you, you attach a general label to them: "He's a loser."

Example: *You make a mistake on a form you filled out, and it's sent back to you in the post. So, you decide, "I'm such a loser" or, "I'm so stupid" rather than thinking, "I made a mistake as I had a busy day when I was filling this out".*

Example 2: *"I didn't stand up to my co-worker, I'm such a wimp!"*

Chapter in a nutshell

- CBT is based on the concept that your thoughts, feelings, physical sensations and actions are interconnected, and that negative thoughts and feelings can trap you in a vicious cycle.
- Graded exposure is when you gently expose yourself to your fear, little by little.
- Your ANTs are your automatic negative thoughts. Pesky little things that need stamping on!
- Thought traps are patterns of distorted thinking. The most common are:
- All or nothing thinking
- Over-generalising
- Filtering out the positive and focusing on the negatives
- Mind reading and fortune telling
- Catastrophising
- Emotional reasoning
- Musturbation
- Labelling
- Taking the blame for everything

Actions

- Understand your patterns of distorted thinking and write them down, so you are more likely to recognise them as they come up throughout the day. Download a template for recognising your own ANTs at www.jorichings.com/whoops

CHOOSING MORE HELPFUL THOUGHTS

"People are not disturbed by things, but by the view they take of them." –Epictetus

The idea that we have the power to choose our thoughts is not a new one. Buddhists have been saying the same thing for thousands of years.

The more you focus on unhelpful thoughts, the more frustrated you will become with yourself and your life. We all have moments of self-doubt. Your chimp will always be on high alert for danger – that's his job. Your job is to recognise when your chimp thinking is unhelpful and learn to mentally "tune out" by shifting your attention elsewhere.

The less attention you pay to your unhelpful thoughts, the less receptive you will be to them over time. You wouldn't leave the television on showing a programme that made you feel awful, would you? You'd simply turn the channel over to something more enjoyable, and not give the previous channel even a backward glance.

The first step to choosing more helpful thoughts is to turn up your internal volume and listen to what you say to yourself on a daily basis. Be super aware of your negative thoughts and beliefs.

Whenever you start to think negatively, stop and think a

more helpful thought. Do something different. The idea is to interrupt the pattern and replace the negative thought process with a more helpful one.

Interrupting the Pattern

There are various ways that you can choose to "interrupt the pattern". Here are some of the ideas that have worked for me.

- Delete Delete. This simple NLP (neuro-linguistic programming) technique involves tapping a point on your body and saying "delete, delete" each time you catch yourself thinking or talking negatively. Then replace it with a more helpful thought.

- Whiteboard. Imagine your mind is like a whiteboard, and you are erasing the thought from it. See the new, more helpful thought written on your board.

- Tap. Simply tap on the side of your fingernail while saying your new thought.

- Distraction. Get up, put some music on, sing, dance, jump around like a mad person – anything that changes your physiology.

- Challenge the thought. Is it true? What evidence do you have that it's true? What evidence do you have that it's not true? How could you look at this differently?

- Phone a friend. Well, you are not really going to phone a friend, but you can still ask yourself whether you would speak to a friend in the same way, using the same language. If the answer is no, then stop talking to yourself in this way. Be your own best friend.

- Smile and simply be aware that your chimp is worried and wants to run the show. Tell him or her that you've got this and that you are choosing to think in a more helpful way. Tell your chimp, "Thanks but back off" – you've got this.

The more you do this, the easier it will become. When you choose to think the new, more helpful thought, you are creating a new neural pathway in your brain, which becomes deeper through repetition. The deeper the "groove", the more of a habit this way of thinking will become.

Here is a list of more helpful thoughts to counteract some of the more popular unhelpful beliefs and thoughts. Download the template at www.jorichings.com/whoops. Tick the ones that you have heard yourself using. Star the ones you hear yourself saying a lot.

I'm so stupid

I may not be able to do this YET, but I will.

She's much better than me

She may find it easier than me, but I find other things easier than her.

I can't deal with this

I've done tricky things in the past. I know I can do this if I take my time.

I always make mistakes

Everyone makes mistakes sometimes. That's OK. I tried my best, and that's what counts.

I'm no good at this

I may find this difficult right now, but by taking small steps, I'll learn every day.

I'm too shy

What's the worst that can happen? Whatever it is, I can cope with it. I can do this!

I can't do it; I'm no good

I don't have to be good at everything. I'm challenging myself which helps me grow.

I messed that up

Nobody is perfect. We all mess up sometimes.

I'm not very confident

I'm getting a little more confident every day.

I'm fat

OK, so I get that the more I think like that the worse I'll feel. How about I give myself a break and stop saying that?

I've always been like this

That's because I've always thought the same way. Thinking differently about this can help me change.

I can't

What if I could? I can try. I can learn, and I can practise. Saying "I can't" won't help.

Nothing ever works out for me

I bet if I tried I could think of lots of things that have worked out for me. Let's not think like that.

I should be doing better in life

OK, so what would I like to be better at? What do I need to do to be better?

It will never get any better

Maybe it could be a little better? What small steps could I take to improve the situation?

I can't forgive him/her

Not forgiving is a little like swallowing poison and hoping the other person will get sick. I'm only hurting myself. I can try to let it go...

It's too much for me

I can handle this. I can break it down into bite-sized chunks and deal with one piece at a time.

I'm useless

OK, so that didn't go as well as I wanted, but I can and will do better next time.

They're horrible to me

OK, so they aren't nice. I can't control them, but I CAN choose not to let them bother me.

I always forget

Actually, that's not really true. I don't always forget. I can remember lots of things.

I always mess it up

I'm just thinking that because I'm nervous. Back off chimp, I've got this!

I'm not confident enough

I'm getting a little more confident every day. Confidence is a skill I can learn.

I can't cope

OK, take a deep breath. That's just my chimp talking. Relax. We've got this!

I feel like a failure

Everyone messes up sometimes. That's OK. I can just pick myself up and try again.

I never do anything right

If I remind myself what I've done well every day, then my confidence will grow.

I wouldn't be any good at that

Telling myself, "I can't" means I won't be able to. I choose to think positively. I may be good at this: I won't know until I try.

I'm frustrated

Thinking that isn't going to help, is it? It will only make me more frustrated. How else can I approach this?

It's not my fault

Sometimes it's too easy to blame other people or situations.

What could I have done differently?

It's too hard

Thinking like that is only going to make it harder. How about I think "this is getting a little easier" instead?

I always... I never...

Sentences that I start with "always" or "never" are probably not helping me!

I should

"I should" is usually followed by something I don't want to do! How about I say, "I can" or "'I will" instead?

Why can't I do anything right?

Actually, I do a lot of things right. This thing may just need a little more practice.

What if......?

In the words of Mark Twain, "I've been through some really terrible things in my life SOME OF WHICH actually happened!" Let's not go there...

Everybody hates me

Not everyone hates me. I have friends and family who like me.

Everyone thinks I'm stupid

No, I'm sure they don't. I need to remember all the great things I like about myself and ignore that chimp!

I always get it wrong

Everyone makes mistakes. Mistakes just mean I'm learning and challenging myself.

I'm going to make a fool of myself

I'm going to do my best, and that's the best I can do!

I'm terrible at that

OK, so I may not be an expert, but I don't have to be good at everything. I can get better at anything if I practise.

I shout a lot when I'm angry

I can't control other people or situations, but I can control my response.

I keep losing control

My chimp thinks I'm in danger. But I'm not! I'm OK. I've got this.

I often react badly

I'm in control of my emotions. Nobody else. I know I can choose a different response.

Nothing seems to work

OK, so this is not working right now. Let's try looking at it differently. Who can I ask for help?

I'm not good enough

That's not being very kind to myself. Would I say that to anyone else?

I'll never change

Well, if I carry on thinking like that I won't! What if I could change? Do I want to change? I can change if I want to.

Nobody likes me

Not everyone will like me, just like I don't have to like everyone. That's OK. There are people that like me.

He thinks I'm ugly

Actually, I don't really know what he's thinking. I'm not a mind reader! And I accept myself just the way I am anyway.

There's so much that could go wrong

Yes, things could go wrong but let's think about what could go right.

I'm so mad/angry

I could use one of the techniques I've learned to calm myself down. Take a few deep breaths, listen to my helpful thoughts playlist or try some tapping.

I'm going to fail

If I tell myself I'll fail, I'm not giving myself much of a chance. I can do this.

Chapter in a nutshell

- The more you focus on unhelpful thoughts, the more frustrated you will become with yourself and your life.

- Your chimp will always be on high alert for danger – that's his job. Your job is to recognise when your chimp thinking is unhelpful and learn to mentally "tune out" by shifting your attention elsewhere.

- Turn up your internal volume and listen to what you say to yourself.

- Interrupt the pattern:

  - Delete, delete.

  - Tap. Distraction.

  - Challenge the thought.

  - Phone a friend.

- Be aware that your chimp is running the show.

- Be aware of your most common unhelpful thoughts.

- Replace them with more helpful ways of thinking.

Actions

- Identify your most unhelpful thoughts and list your alternative, more helpful thoughts. Recognise when your chimp is running the show.

- Download the HappiMe app, create yourself a playlist of helpful thoughts and listen as often as you can!

AMAZING AFFIRMATIONS

"It's the repetition of affirmations that leads to belief. And once that belief becomes a deep conviction, things begin to happen"
–Muhammad Ali

According to the dictionary, affirmations are "the action or process of affirming something".

Positive affirmations are simple, short, positive statements, said repeatedly. Like helpful thoughts, they are aimed at changing your mindset or your beliefs in a particular area. Many people are already very good at negative affirmations, and unfortunately, most don't realise that these negative affirmations are shaping their lives.

The difference between an affirmation and a helpful thought is that an affirmation tends to be a very positive thought and a helpful thought is just a little better than your current way of thinking.

If a positive affirmation is too far away from where you are right now for your subconscious mind to accept it, it is unlikely to be successful.

Examples of negative affirmations / unhelpful thinking.	Examples of more helpful thoughts.	Examples of positive affirmations.
I am always late.	I am getting better at being on time.	I am always on time.
I am rubbish at my job.	I am improving every day.	I am great at my job.
I can't cook.	I am learning to be a better cook.	I am a good cook.
I hate exercise.	I am beginning to like exercise.	I enjoy exercise.
I can't control my eating habits.	Every day it is getting easier to be in control of my eating habits.	I am in control of my eating habits.

If saying a helpful thought in the present tense is too difficult to believe then your chimp will often reject the new belief. He or she will be saying something along the lines of, "Really? No that's never going to happen/you can't do that/what about all the times you failed before?"

If the helpful thought makes you feel uncomfortable anywhere in your body or your chimp pipes up loudly every time you say or listen to it, then choose helpful thoughts like, "I am becoming, I am on my way, I have the potential, I choose to, every day I am getting..."

As you know, your subconscious mind is like a computer,

running its various programmes quietly in the background. Every belief you have about yourself and the world around you, whether that is good, bad or indifferent, is a programme in your computer that is affecting your everyday behaviour. It controls everything from our level of confidence or skill levels, our ability to lose weight, keep at an exercise programme, our ability to be successful and a million other things. Your mind is designed to work towards whatever you think about – good, bad, or indifferent. It doesn't know good from bad or right from wrong. It will just do what you tell it to do.

Listen to or say your helpful thoughts as often as you can.

This is probably the most important point and where most people fall down. Many experts tell you to repeat your affirmations twice a day in front of the mirror but, as discussed, we have anywhere between 30,000-60,000 thoughts a day, and most of those thoughts are negative, self-sabotaging thoughts.

Standing in front of the mirror repeating your affirmations or helpful thoughts twice a day is just not going to cut it. This is the main reason why the HappiMe app was designed: To give people an easy way to listen to personalised helpful thoughts – that resonate and that the mind can accept – over and over again. If you are saying or listening to your affirmations 100 times a day but talk and think negatively for the rest of the day, things are not going to change.

Sometimes affirmations or helpful thoughts are just not enough...

When we have a deep-rooted negative belief, choosing more helpful thoughts or affirmations on their own are just not enough. Take weight loss for example. Many people have deep emotional reasons why they overeat and listening to affirmations without tackling the cause behind the negative behaviour is a little like putting a sticking plaster on a gaping wound or standing in a weedy garden shouting "weeds don't grow". It is not going to work! Time for the heavy duty weed killer – bring on the EFT!

Chapter in a nutshell

- Positive affirmations are simple, short, positive statements, said repeatedly.

- Choose thoughts and affirmations that your chimp will accept.

- You have 30,000-60,000 thoughts a day, most of them negative.

Actions

- Listen or say your affirmations as often as you can.

HEAVY DUTY WEED KILLER AKA EMOTIONAL FREEDOM TECHNIQUE (EFT)

"Willpower can produce short-term change, but it creates constant internal stress because you haven't dealt with the cause." –Rick Warren

Pretty much everyone I have ever worked with has had stuff to deal with. Stuff is the reason why we self-sabotage, the reason why we overeat, drink too much or spend most of our lives worrying. Our stuff is why we feel that we are not good enough. Our stuff is what stops us going after our dreams.

It's the negative and self-sabotaging beliefs that we hold. More often than not, these beliefs will stem from something that happened to us in our childhood. And it doesn't necessarily have to be anything particularly traumatic.

Imagine putting up your hand in class and getting the answer wrong. All your classmates laugh. You are mortified. You are so embarrassed. Your chimp brain, the part of your brain in charge of keeping you safe, will be thinking, "Gosh, that was stupid. Everyone laughed. They think I am an idiot. I'm not good enough". This can be all it takes to create a belief that you are not good enough.

On the other hand, our stuff could be the awful, traumatic experiences we have had. Like child abuse or neglect. Or experiencing our parents going through a horrific divorce.

Most of what we believe to be true about ourselves and the world around us is formed by the time we are five or six years old. These beliefs come from either our own experiences or through blind acceptance of what other people tell us. The way our parents, grandparents, teachers, siblings and family friends treat us has a significant impact on what we believe to be true about ourselves.

I'm Not Good Enough

I can remember my Dad asking me what I wanted to do when I grew up. I think I was about eight or nine. I told him I wanted to be Prime Minister and he said, "That's a great start, what do you want to do after that?" On the surface, this sounds like a positive and supportive response. To my eight-year-old chimp, it sounded like a criticism. "Goodness me, even being Prime Minister isn't good enough. That means I am not good enough. Must try harder to be good enough."

This led to a lifetime of driving myself to be, do and have more. Nothing was ever enough. I had to do more. The positive from Dad's parenting style was that it drove me to have a very successful career, but it came at a cost. Forty years of feeling not good enough was exhausting, not to mention the impact that it had on my relationships. I don't blame him in any way for this though – he was just doing what he thought was best at the time.

The belief that you're not good enough is a fear routine that affects nearly everyone, though it shows up differently for each person. For some of you, "not good enough" will express itself as it did for me – by going into workaholic overachiever mode; for others, it shows up as comparisons; for others, it shows up as procrastination, avoidance and not finishing what you start.

I believe that the fastest way to get rid of deep-rooted fears or anxieties is EFT.

EFT (Emotional Freedom Technique), Tapping or HappiTapping as we call it on the HappiMe app, is simply acupuncture without the needles. It uses the same energy meridians from traditional acupuncture to treat physical and emotional ailments, but instead of inserting needles, you simply tap the acupressure points with your fingertips.

At the same time as you tap, you talk about what is causing the negative emotion or problem, finishing the tapping sequence with positive affirmations to help you overcome the problem. This process quickly and easily releases any negative emotions and feelings associated with the problem. The tapping motion releases tension by sending messages to your chimp brain that everything is OK.

So far, EFT has been researched in more than ten countries, by more than 60 investigators, whose results have been published in more than 20 different peer-reviewed journals. These include distinguished top-tier journals such as Journal of Clinical Psychology, the APA journals Psychotherapy: Theory, Research, Practice, Training and Review of General Psychology, and the oldest psychiatric journal in North America, the Journal of Nervous and Mental Disease. You can read this research at www.happi-me.org/science-behind-happitapping

These trials have demonstrated that EFT is effective for phobias, grief, anxiety, depression, post-traumatic stress disorder (PTSD), pain, and many other problems. Today, over nine million people a month search online for "EFT tapping".

When I first came across EFT I was sceptical – it sounds a

little weird after all. But EFT kept coming up on my radar, and as I have this deal with the universe about paying attention when I see something three times in quick succession, I decided to research it thoroughly.

As I mentioned in Part One, in 2013 I was lucky enough to spend a month out in Bali on an entrepreneur's retreat. (Yes, it was as incredible as it sounds!) I bought a book called *The Tapping Solution* to read on the flight over. I was blown away by what I was reading. If it was true, it was incredible. Guess who was one of the first people I met on the retreat in Bali? A very gifted EFT practitioner. What are the chances? There were 12 of us on the retreat, and one just happened to be an fantastic EFT practitioner. Don't you just love the synchronicities of life? Helga and I did a lot of EFT during that month, and it really was life-changing. I cleared the trauma from my childhood, my grief over losing my mum and my anger at having cancer. It's hard to explain, but I felt such an incredible internal shift.

Since then I have researched EFT extensively and found the results it's getting around the world astonishing. I have used it myself to clear my deep-rooted issues around my weight and really can't recommend it highly enough. In fact, I do to pretty much all my clients. I have watched EFT clear phobias, grief and anxiety in just a few sessions.

As you can tell I am a massive advocate for EFT – it is one of the most exciting therapies I have come across in the last ten years. In case you are not convinced, here are 16 reasons why I think everyone should learn EFT!

1. Tapping is free, needs no equipment and is easy to learn.

2. It only takes a few minutes to learn how to do it.

3. Anyone can learn to tap, even kids.

4. It's easy to teach to friends and family.

5. With EFT, you become responsible for soothing or calming yourself, instead of waiting for another person to change their mood, attitude or behaviour so that you can feel better.

6. It's a great tool to calm or soothe yourself emotionally, mentally and/or physically.

7. It can be done anywhere (i.e. in the bathroom when you are with others or out in a public place). If you can't find a private place to do a few rounds of tapping, EFT can be easily modified, i.e. just tap on karate chop or finger tapping on the side of the fingers.

8. It is fantastic for eliminating cravings.

9. It can help relieve physical pain.

10. Tapping is a powerful tool for disease prevention. Trapped negative energy in the body like stress, tension, anxiety and worry has been clinically proven to lead to illness such as ulcers, Crohn's disease, colitis, chronic stress disorder, back problems, migraines, tension headaches, fibromyalgia, IBS, chronic fatigue syndrome and mood disorders such as depression.

11. It can get rid of phobias and fears within 45 minutes.

12. Use it to get rid of negative thoughts and beliefs.

13. It can help you deal with guilt, grief, stress, worrying, childhood trauma.

14. It can improve your self-esteem and boost your confidence.

15. It's entirely safe; no one has ever been harmed by tapping.

16. The least that can happen is that you'll feel a little more relaxed and calm after doing a few rounds of tapping.

How Do We Do It?

(You can watch videos on how to tap at www.happi-me.org/happitapping-videos-for-adults)

Firstly, ask yourself these four simple questions:

1. What's the problem you'd like to deal with?

2. What emotion do you feel?

3. Where do you feel it?

4. What number is it? Rate the emotion you're feeling on a scale of 1 to 10 (10 being high).

Create Your Set Up Statement

Use the four questions above to create your set up statement.

For example:

Problem: Meeting with the boss (1)

Emotion: Anxiousness (2)

Location: Sick feeling in my stomach (3)

Rate from 1-10: 8/10 (4)

Start your set up statement with *"Even though..."* and end with a positive statement like *"I love and accept myself anyway..."* or: *I'm a good person and deserve to be happy".*

Gently tap on the fleshy part between the side of your little finger and wrist.

Even though I am feeling anxious because I have a meeting with my boss and it's making me feel sick to my stomach, I still love and accept myself.

Then tap on the 16 points, while saying how you feel.

Karate point:	Set up statement x 2
Top of the head:	I am feeling anxious,
Between the eyes:	I don't want to have this meeting,
Side of the eye: uncomfortable,	It's making me feel
Under the eye:	I feel sick,
Under the nose:	I don't want to do it,
On your chin:	But I know I'm going to be OK,
Collarbone:	It will be over soon,
Pulse point on wrist:	I am good at my job,
Wrist:	There is nothing to worry about,
Side of nail bed – thumb:	It will be over before I know it,
Side of nail – 1st finger:	I'm releasing this anxiousness,
Side of nail – 2nd finger:	I'm going to be OK,

Side of nail – 3rd finger: I'm feeling better,

Side of nail – little finger: I will get there,

Karate point: I'm letting it go

Check in with yourself; has your number gone down? Repeat the above until your rating is as low as possible.

If you have deeper "stuff" to shift, there are some links to some excellent EFT practitioners that I refer to on the website. (www.happi-me.org/tapping-practitioners.html)

They all work via Skype, so it doesn't matter where you are in the world.

You will also find some helpful tapping videos on the HappiMe app, to help with stress, anxiety, disappointment, sadness and lack of confidence. There are also thousands of YouTube videos with scripts on everything from depression, fear, pain, stress, weight loss, insomnia and clearing negative beliefs.

Although you can learn to tap quickly, you may need the help of an EFT practitioner to clear the deep-rooted stuff.

Chapter in a nutshell

- Tapping is one of the most exciting therapies discovered in the last ten years.

- Our "stuff" is the reason why we self-sabotage.

- Most of what we believe to be true about ourselves and the world around us is formed by the time we are five or six years old.

- The fastest way to get rid of deep-rooted fears or anxieties is EFT.

- Tapping is simply acupuncture without the needles.

- The tapping motion releases tension by sending messages to your chimp brain that everything is OK.

- Tapping is entirely safe, free, needs no equipment and it only takes a few minutes to learn how to do it. Anyone can learn to tap, even kids. It is fantastic for eliminating cravings, relieving physical pain, preventing disease, reducing pain, guilt, stress, and anxiety, clearing phobias, fears, childhood trauma, negative thoughts, and beliefs, improving self-esteem and boosting confidence.

Actions

- Clear your stuff with EFT!

- Watch the tapping videos on the HappiMe app to help with stress, anxiety, disappointment, sadness and lack of confidence.

- You may need the help of an EFT practitioner to clear deep-rooted trauma.

MARVELLOUS MINDFULNESS

"Mindfulness is the aware, balanced acceptance of the present experience. It isn't more complicated than that. It is opening to or receiving the present moment, pleasant or unpleasant, just as it is, without either clinging to it or rejecting it." –Sylvia Boorstein

If I told you that there is one simple thing you could do each day that would make you happier, less anxious, calmer, sharper and more creative and that not only was it free, but you could do it anytime, anywhere alongside whatever else you are doing – would you do it?

Well, you would think the answer to that would be a resounding yes, wouldn't you? But alas, unfortunately not. Mindfulness often seems to fall in the same category as "take the stairs, not the lift", "drink more water" and "eat less sugar". It's something we sort of know is good for us, but we still don't do. Chimp sabotage at its best!

There is a huge amount of evidence for the benefits of mindfulness. It reduces the impact of stress, anxiety and low moods, and has even been proven to be as effective as antidepressants for depression.

The Science Behind Mindfulness

A simple Google search into the science behind mindfulness shows up over 700,000 results. Multiple scientific studies have shown that mindfulness positively affects the brain patterns underlying day-to-day anxiety, stress, depression, and irritability so that when they arise, they dissolve away again more easily. Now promoted by the NHS as a recommended route to mental wellbeing, mindfulness has also been shown to improve memory, increase creativity and your reaction times become faster.

A study at the University of Pittsburgh showed that MRI scans taken after an eight-week course of mindfulness practice showed that the brain's "fight or flight" centre, the amygdala (your chimp brain), appears to shrink.

As the amygdala shrinks, the prefrontal cortex – associated with higher order brain functions such as awareness, concentration, and decision-making – becomes thicker. The connection between the amygdala and the rest of the brain gets weaker, while the connections between areas associated with attention and concentration get stronger.

Like EFT, practising mindfulness is a great strategy to help quieten your chimp. Chimp thinking often comes in the form of ANTs (automatic negative thoughts).

Mindfulness helps you to be become more present and more aware, especially of your ANTs and the endless chatter in your mind.

"What day is it?" asked Pooh. "It's today," squeaked Piglet. "My favourite day," said Pooh.

Lost in your Thinking Mind

In 2010, researchers at Harvard established that we spend an average of 46.9% of our waking hours thinking about something other than what we are doing. In other words, we are lost in our thinking minds. That's nearly half of our day, two weeks out of every month, six months of every year. Half of our lives are spent ruminating, worrying and daydreaming! And this mind-wandering typically makes us unhappy.

Mindlessness

Have you ever:

- Started eating a meal, taken a couple of mouthfuls, then suddenly noticed you had pretty much cleared your plate? Or ate without noticing textures and flavours?

- Had an accident because of carelessness, inattention or thinking about something else?

- Read a few sentences and been unable to remember what you just read?

- Forgot someone's name as soon as you hear it? Listened to someone with one ear while doing something else at the same time?

- Rushed to get something done without paying attention to the process of doing it?

- Daydreamed or thought of other things when doing chores?

- Done several things at once rather than focusing on one thing at a time?

- Distracted yourself with things like eating, alcohol, drugs, work?

- Been unable or unwilling to notice and accept uncomfortable emotions or sensations?

- Arrived home from work and remembered nothing about your drive home?

Most people have experienced one or even all of these. These are common examples of "mindlessness", or "going on automatic pilot".

Busy, modern day life means it can be easy to rush through our day without stopping to notice much. We juggle the kids, work, relationships, finances, housework. We are constantly multi-tasking. We are easily distracted, constantly examining past events and trying to anticipate the future.

So much so that we are often not present in our own lives. We fail to notice the good things in our day. We don't notice the fantastic world we live in. We don't hear the birds or see the beautiful flowers. We miss the little loving gestures that loved ones can make. We don't see the signs that all is not well around us. We fail to hear what our bodies are telling us – we miss our early warning alarm signals. We live in our heads. Forever caught up in our thoughts, without stopping to notice how those thoughts are driving our emotions and behaviour.

Becoming more aware of our thoughts, feelings and sensations may not sound like an obviously helpful thing to do, however learning to do this in a way that suspends judgement and self-criticism can have an incredibly positive impact on our lives.

Mindfulness is a way of paying attention to and seeing clearly, whatever is happening in our lives. It's about reconnecting with our bodies and the sensations they experience. This means waking up to the sights, sounds, smells and tastes of the present moment. That might be something as simple as the feel of water on our hands as we wash the dishes. It will not eliminate life's pressures, but it can help us respond to them in a calmer way that benefits our heart, soul, body and mind.

Practising mindfulness doesn't need to take up a lot of your time. In fact, you can fit it into your day to day life easily.

9 Simple Mindfulness Exercises

1. Focus on your Breathing.

Try this exercise anytime you are waiting in a queue, for the kettle to boil or when you are waiting at the traffic lights.

- Focus your full attention on your breath as it flows in and out of your body.

- Notice how fast or slow your breathing is.

- Feel your breath in your nostrils.

- Notice how your chest and stomach moves as you breathe.

Focusing on each breath in this way allows you to observe your thoughts as they arise in your mind. Little by little, you learn to let go of struggling with them, and you realise that thoughts come and go of their own accord. And that you are not your thoughts.

2. Walking Meditation.

- Concentrate on the sensation of your feet touching the ground.

- Notice how you are breathing.

- Look around and *really* notice your surroundings.

- What can you see, hear, feel, smell and taste?

3. Notice the Everyday.

As we go about our daily lives, we can become more aware of what is going on around us.

- Feel the sun on your face.

- Notice the shape of the clouds.

- Hear the wind in the trees.

All this may sound very small, but it has huge power to interrupt the "autopilot" mode we often engage in day to day, and it helps to give us new perspectives on life.

4. The Eating Meditation

When you take the first bite of any meal, just take a moment to pay attention to the taste.

- Look at the food carefully, feel the textures in your mouth, smell it and notice how your body reacts to it.

You don't need to keep this up all the way through the meal but use it every now and then to focus your attention.

5. Name Your Thoughts and Feelings

To develop an awareness of thoughts and feelings, try silently naming them: "Here's the thought that I might fail that exam." Or, "This is anxiety".

- Watch as thoughts appear in your mind, seemingly from thin air, and watch again as they disappear, like a soap bubble bursting.

You will begin to understand that thoughts and feelings (including negative ones) are transient. They come, and they go, and ultimately, you have a choice about whether to act on them or not. You can choose the thoughts you feed.

6. Mindful Brushing

Some things we do so often that we almost don't notice them anymore. Habits, like brushing your teeth, are usually performed automatically, while the mind skips off to other plans, worries or regrets.

Instead, try to *really* focus on brushing your teeth.

- Really experience it. How do you brush your teeth? Do you start at the top or bottom? Left, or right? Is it the same way each time?

- Try brushing your teeth with your opposite hand. How does that feel?

- Notice how the brush moves over your teeth.

- Notice the taste of the toothpaste.

- Simply bring your mind back when it wanders off to other worries or thoughts.

7. Three Mindful Breaths

This exercise can be done standing up or sitting down, and pretty much anywhere at any time. All you need to do is be still and focus on your breath for three mindful breaths. My wonderful friend and Mindfulness teacher, Jackie Hawken, taught me that the best time to do this exercise is when you go to the loo, as most of us do this a few times a day!

- Simply take a deep breath and as you inhale say to yourself. "I am breathing in" and as you exhale slowly, say to yourself "I am breathing out".

Do this three times to feel instantly more relaxed.

8. Mindful Listening

In any conversation, you can use the person that's speaking as your "object of mindfulness".

- Pay full attention to what he or she is saying.

- When your mind wanders away from what is being said, immediately and without judgement bring yourself back to the words of the person speaking.

- Repeat those instructions as many times as necessary.

You will eventually strengthen your mindfulness muscle, allowing you to stay more focused and aware.

9. The Body Scan

Try this lovely mindfulness exercise as you are going off to sleep.

- Firstly, focus on your breath, noticing the rhythm. Don't try to change it – just be aware of your breath as you inhale and exhale.

- Next, become aware of your body and how it feels in your bed.

- Notice the temperature of your body.

- Then, scan your body from head to toe, noticing how each part of your body feels. Again, without judgement. Just notice how each part feels.

Over time, mindfulness brings about long-term changes in mood and levels of happiness and wellbeing.

Myth of Mindfulness

Myth #1: Mindfulness conflicts with certain religions.

There's no belief system connected to mindfulness, even as it was originally taught by the Buddha. Mindfulness is not a religion but simply a tool for wellbeing, and can be practised by anyone, no matter what your belief system.

Myth #2: We need to be present in the moment ALL the time.

It isn't a goal of mindfulness to be present in each and every moment.

Myth #3: Mindfulness is just about emptying your mind, what's the point?

For starters, emptying your mind doesn't really ever happen. What a frustrating practice this would be if that were the case! The brain's job is to continually generate thoughts, so to try and stop or suppress that would be a futile endeavour. The brain doesn't have an off switch. Thoughts will inevitably arise, no matter how good you become at mindfulness.

Myth #4: Mindfulness is easy.

Sometimes it's easy, and sometimes it's not. The biggest challenge can be remembering to be mindful! It does get easier with practice, like any habit, as you create new neural pathways in your brain.

Myth #5: Mindfulness is boring.

It's not boring to carve out time to be by yourself, and you might find the process of realising how much your thoughts have been controlling you, and how much of life you've been missing by not being in the present moment, not only fascinating but can also be fun. If anything, mindfulness is surprising – you learn a lot about yourself.

Myth #6: Mindfulness and mindfulness meditation is the same thing.

No, it's not. Mindfulness can be practised in two ways; formally through mindfulness meditation and informally during the daily events of our lives.

"In today's rush, we all think too much — seek too much — want too much — and forget about the joy of just being." – Eckhart Tolle

Chapter in a nutshell

- Mindfulness reduces anxiety and stress levels and improves sleep and concentration. You can practise mindfulness anywhere.

- Practising mindfulness helps you to be aware of your ANTs – the automatic negative thoughts from your chimp.

- Mindfulness slows you down long enough for you to smell the roses. To notice the fantastic world that you live in.

9 Simple Mindfulness Exercises

1. Focus on your Breathing
2. Walking Meditation
3. Notice the Everyday
4. The Eating Meditation
5. Name Your Thoughts and Feelings
6. Mindful Brushing
7. Three Mindful Breaths
8. Mindful Listening
9. The Body Scan

Actions

- Choose a different mindfulness exercise to do each day.

- Listen to one of the mindful bites on the HappiMe app.

- Become mindful of your chimp's ANT's.

LEVERAGE

"The first step toward change is awareness. The second step is acceptance." –Nathaniel Branden

Leverage is a very useful tool when you are looking to make positive changes in your life. In this chapter, you are going to think about the impact and likely consequences your negative beliefs or worrying have had on your life so far.

Please don't skip this exercise. Many of us are in denial about the impact our negative thinking has had on our lives so far and refuse to think about what will happen if we continue doing what we have always done. We kid ourselves that we are "happy as we are". I am pretty sure you are not happy as you are. If you were, you probably wouldn't be reading this book.

"If you always do what you have always done, you will always get what you have always got." –Tony Robbins

I want you to seriously consider what your belief system has stopped you doing in the past. How has it impacted your life? What have been the consequences? What have you missed out on?

Here are some of mine in relation to my weight...

The impact my weight had on my life:

- I was bullied for being fat which led to even lower self-esteem and choosing the wrong men throughout my life, believing deep down that I wasn't really worth anything better.

- People made judgements about me because of my weight. Whether you like it or not, there are people out there that will think that you are lazy and stupid because you have "allowed" yourself to gain weight and "get fat".

- Buying clothes was a nightmare. I could only buy clothes online or in old-fashioned plus-size shops. I hated dressing rooms with a vengeance. Black clothes were my best friend. I guess we all kid ourselves that we look "slimmer" in black. Not true... 280 pounds looks like 280 pounds whatever colour you are wearing (except maybe horizontal stripes, then it may look like 300 pounds).

- I refused to go on holiday abroad for years because, not only would I have to wear a swimming costume at some point, I would also have to wear strappy dresses that showed my flabby arms (unless I was going to wear a shrug in 30-degree heat). Not to mention that I was worried I wouldn't fit into the plane seat in the first place. When I flew to Florida in 2010 I had to ask for a seatbelt extension. It was one of the most embarrassing moments of my life. I also knew that even if I could fit in the plane seat, I wouldn't be able to put the food tray down as my tummy would be in the way.

- My weight impacted on how I played with my kids. Running around kicking a ball was just not an option. Neither were fairground rides.

- I believe that my food choices and weight were a contributing factor to my breast cancer.

- My weight and poor body image stopped me getting naked with my partners.

- I was embarrassed, disappointed and disgusted with myself. I felt that if I didn't lose weight I would lose my integrity as a coach. How the hell could I tell people that they could achieve anything they wanted if I couldn't lose weight?

OK, your turn...

What is the one key area of your life you would like to change?

What are the self-limiting beliefs that are holding you back?

What has your belief system stopped you doing?

Finding a new partner?

Ditching the old partner?

Changing career?

Starting a business?

Being happy?

Accepting yourself?

Having exciting experiences?

Going after that promotion?

Be honest.

Really think about how that makes you feel. Dig into the

emotion.

List at least 5-10 ways that this has impacted your life negatively.

Next, explore what will happen if you don't change now. What happens if you carry on thinking the same way? Describe your life in 5 years. What will you look like? Will you be more anxious? Unhappier? Unhealthier? What impact will this have on your life?

Here were some of my thoughts...

- If I don't start looking after myself then cancer may kill me before the five years are up. My kids won't have a Mum to look out for them. No one to love them unconditionally. To be a positive influence on their lives. I won't live to see my grandchildren. Mum and Dad will have to bury their daughter.

- Even if the cancer doesn't return, I won't ever want to fly again for fear of not fitting in the seats, so I will miss out on wonderful holidays abroad. I will have trouble moving about. I will miss out on lots of amazing experiences

What will you miss out on if you keep thinking the same way? Love? A great career? Healthier relationships? A healthy body?

Now go forward ten years and do the same...

- That one was easy for me. If I happened still to be here, I was likely to have a whole new plethora of diseases, such as diabetes, heart disease, breathing difficulties and joint problems.

20 years….

I honestly believed if I had kept going along the same path of overeating, not exercising and being constantly stressed, there was no way I would still be here in 20 years.

Don't just do this exercise in your head. Write it down in your notebook. It's a powerful exercise that will help build your willpower muscle when things are tough and your chimp is on your back.

Please… don't skip it. Recognise that your chimp will not want you to go there, so he or she is likely to be telling you one of the following right now:

"Oh dear, we haven't got a pen. Best do it later."

"We don't really want to write in the book and I don't know where the pad is."

"We can just think it through in our minds. We don't need to write it down."

"I can't see how that will help – let's skip this bit. We can always come back to it."

Nooooooo. Don't listen. You are wise to sneaky chimp ways. Do it now! Your future happiness may depend on it.

Chapter in a nutshell

- Leverage is a very useful tool when you are looking to make positive changes in your life.

- Think about the impact and negative consequences your negative beliefs have had on your life so far.

- Decide which key area of your life you would like to change.

- Understand the impact your current way of thinking has had on this area of your life so far, and what will happen in the future if you do not change this belief or behaviour.

- Be prepared for chimp sabotage.

Actions

- Do the exercise! No, really – do the exercise.

GOALS AND DREAMS. PURPOSE AND PASSION

"Setting goals is the first step in turning the invisible into the visible" –Tony Robbins

By now, I trust that you are starting to believe that it is possible to change the way you think and that when you are the Master of your Mind, absolutely anything is possible.

I honestly believe that everyone is capable of far more than they realise. I also believe that we all deserve to live happy, more fulfilled lives. Unfortunately, most people will go through life believing that this is just not true for them. They settle. They justify. And give up on their dreams.

I challenge you to start dreaming again.

What would you like to be different in your life? If failure wasn't an option, what would you do? If you could wake up tomorrow in your dream life, what would be different? Would you be in the same job or business? Same relationship? Same weight or fitness level? Would you live in the same place with the same people? Would you have new friends, new hobbies? Would you travel? Start a business? Learn a new skill?

Start to think about what you would like to Be, Do and Have in life. Write your "101 bucket list". A list of 101 things you would like to be, do or have before you die.

9 Super Reasons You Should Have a 101 Bucket List:

1. Writing goals down makes you think about what you want from life.

2. According to a study by Dr. Gail Matthews at the Dominican University of California, you are 42% more likely to achieve something that you have written down.

3. Looking at what you have achieved makes you feel great.

4. You are leveraging the Law of Attraction (more on that later).

5. It gives you focus.

6. It keeps you motivated.

7. It's fun and rewarding.

8. It gives you purpose.

9. It gives you direction.

Tips for a creating great 101 lists

- Let your imagination run wild and dream big.

- Think "how can I?" rather than "I can't".

- Don't worry about the how.

- Put dates on your goals, especially the ones you would like to achieve over the next few years.

- Think outside the box. Check out bucketlist.org – it has nearly 6 million goals listed, from ghost hunting to kayaking through caves.

- Target different areas of your life – hobbies, finances, career or business, relationships, etc.

- Make sure you include some easy goals – when we achieve, our bodies release dopamine, a feel-good chemical that spurs us on.

- Don't try to do it all at once. Most people have to come back to it a few times to get to 101.

- Make a list with your partner if you have one, or make a family 101 list and get the kids involved.

- Get pictures of your goals and create a dream board (also a great one to do as a family).

Here are some examples to get you started. The majority of bucket-lists tend to be full of experiences rather than material things that you want to own.

Examples of Be

What kind of person do you want to be?

1. Kind.
2. Hardworking.
3. Friendly.
4. Generous.
5. Loving.
6. A great parent.
7. More patient.
8. More tolerant.
9. Humble.
10. Ambitious.
11. A great manager.
12. Knowledgeable.
13. Funny.
14. The best sibling.

15. Tidy.
16. Accepting.
17. Loyal.
18. Warm.
19. Youthful.
20. An amazing friend.
21. Curious.
22. Organised.
23. Disciplined.
24. Fit.
25. A great son or daughter.
26. Slimmer.
27. Happier.
28. Spontaneous.
29. Empowered.
30. Engaged.
31. Helpful.
32. Honest.
33. Truthful.
34. Alert.
35. Calm.
36. Peaceful.
37. Wild.
38. Wise.
39. Sexy.
40. Conscientious.
41. Easy-going
42. Adventurous.
43. Playful.
44. Cheerful.
45. Mature.
46. Compassionate.
47. Accountable.
48. Punctual.
49. Tasteful.
50. Responsible.
51. Sociable.
52. Empathetic.
53. Healthy.

54. Imaginative.
55. Original.
56. Authentic.
57. Intuitive.
58. Positive.
59. Flexible.
60. Romantic.
61. Educated.
62. Dynamic.
63. Dignified.
64. Elegant.
65. Creative.
66. Daring.
67. Spiritual.
68. Motivational.
69. Courageous.
70. Motivated.
71. Inspirational.
72. Powerful.
73. Sensitive.
74. Content.
75. Outgoing.
76. Driven.
77. Respected.
78. Charismatic.
79. Strong.
80. Enlightened.
81. Sophisticated.
82. Skilful.
83. Vivacious.
84. Balanced.
85. Serious.
86. Confident.
87. Considerate.
88. Sympathetic.
89. Secure.
90. Trusting.
91. Amusing.
92. Understanding.

93. Appreciative.
94. Caring.
95. Witty.
96. Sweet.
97. Stable.
98. Open.
99. Direct.
100. Bold.
101. Determined.

Examples of Do

What kind of things do you want to do?

1. Jump out of a plane.
2. Fly a plane.
3. Drive a train.
4. Base jump.
5. Fall in love.
6. Have a family.
7. Go skiing.
8. Learn to snowboard.
9. Learn to drive.
10. Learn to cook.
11. Learn to dance salsa.
12. Take a line dancing class.
13. Join a gym.
14. Take Zumba classes.
15. Learn to play the guitar.
16. Take drum lessons.
17. Learn a language.
18. Take a class.
19. Start a new hobby.
20. Go to a comedy club.
21. Perform on stage.
22. Act in a play.
23. Start a meetup group.
24. Read a book a month for a year.

25. Go back to college.
26. Go sailing.
27. Go jet skiing.
28. Watch more live music.
29. Sing to an audience.
30. Volunteer.
31. Practise self-care.
32. Travel more.
33. Start a business.
34. Live in another country.
35. Put your children in private education.
36. Buy Gucci shoes.
37. Sleep under the stars.
38. Make love under the stars.
39. Go in a hot air balloon.
40. Develop my spiritual awareness.
41. Teach what I love to another person.
42. Write a book.
43. Enhance someone else's life.
44. Give flowers to a stranger.
45. Grow my own vegetables.
46. Save a life.
47. Practise gratitude daily.
48. Put my feet in the ocean.
49. Eat sushi in Japan.
50. Go on a Segway.
51. Eat Belgian waffles in Belgium.
52. See Big Ben.
53. Kiss under a waterfall.
54. Go on the London Eye.
55. See a Broadway show.
56. Picnic in Central Park.
57. Go camping.
58. Ride a horse.
59. Learn to paint.
60. Ride a camel.
61. Go paintballing.
62. Go to the ballet.
63. Attend a ball.

64. Chase a tornado.
65. Go on a zip line.
66. Float in the Dead Sea.
67. Visit the sex museum in Amsterdam.
68. Be on TV.
69. Learn to swim.
70. Go snorkelling.
71. Climb a mountain.
72. Fly business class.
73. Go to a music festival
74. Ride on the back of a Harley.
75. Travel Route 66.
76. Swim with dolphins.
77. Play the piano.
78. Get married.
79. Have a spa day.
80. Get a tattoo.
81. Go camping.
82. Hike the Grand Canyon.
83. Stay up all night in Vegas.
84. Learn tai chi.
85. Have a fish pedicure.
86. Hang glide.
87. Go on a ghost hunt.
88. Scuba dive.
89. Attend Mardi Gras.
90. Go hiking in the rainforest.
91. Solve a Rubik cube.
92. Meet the Queen.
93. Sleep on the beach.
94. Have a food fight.
95. Go to university.
96. Go on a cruise.
97. Have a pillow fight.
98. Climb the Eiffel Tower.
99. Meet your favourite celebrity.
100. Kayak through caves.
101. Witness an eclipse

Examples of Have

What kind of things do you want to have?

1. A certain make and model of car.
2. An MBE.
3. A dog.
4. Great relationships.
5. A loving family.
6. A tent.
7. A cat.
8. My own home.
9. Savings in the bank.
10. A villa in Spain.
11. A family.
12. Holidays twice a year.
13. A job that I love.
14. A successful business.
15. A better job.
16. A better income.
17. A degree.
18. A horse.
19. My own tribe.
20. A driving licence.
21. Self-respect.
22. A pilot's licence.
23. A MacBook.
24. A new bike.
25. A subscription to my favourite magazine.
26. Happiness.
27. A cleaner.
28. A gardener.
29. A best friend.
30. Peace.
31. My favourite... "insert your stuff".

Then, choose one thing at a time and get to work!

If you don't know how to do it – buy a book, watch a video, go on a course, Google it or find a mentor. Find a way to learn. You have already learned so much in your life.

Take driving a car for example. We quickly forget the considerable skill it takes to drive. We move seamlessly through using the clutch, brakes, accelerator, and indicators while checking rear-view mirrors, wing mirrors, distance from the kerb, obstacles and distance to other vehicles. There is so much to learn, but within months, most of us can drive from a to b on automatic pilot. How many times have you arrived home without any memory of your journey? If you are anything like me, then the answer will be loads. It's pretty scary really.

"Just try new things. Don't be afraid. Step out of your comfort zones and soar." –Michelle Obama

The four stages of learning

Every time we learn something new, we go through the four stages of learning:

1. Unconscious incompetence

Blissful ignorance. We don't know what we don't know.

2. Conscious incompetence

We discover a skill we wish to learn – driving a car, riding a bike. Confidence drops as we realise our ability is limited. We need to practise learning. Often this means not succeeding at first. This is learning; unfortunately, in our culture, it is often labelled "failure". We feel uncomfortable. We know what we don't know.

3. Conscious competence

We acquire the skill. We have become consciously competent. Our conscious mind can only cope with a small number of new bits of information at any one time. Our confidence increases with our ability. We have to concentrate, but we know what to do.

4. Unconscious competence

Lastly, we blend the skills together, and they become habits – we can then do them while our mind is on other things. We have reached the stage of unconscious competence. Our confidence and ability have peaked, we no longer have to concentrate on what we do.

Understanding that you need to go through these four levels to learn any new skill, makes it easier to commit to learning a new skill.

"The expert at anything was once a beginner." –Helen Hayes

The GROW Self-Coaching Model

As much as I would love to, I can't be with you personally every day as your Coach, so I would like to introduce you to a simple, but extremely powerful, self-coaching model called GROW.

The GROW model by Sir John Whitmore is one of the most popular coaching models around and really simple and easy to use.

The G is for Goal.

The first thing do is to set the Goal.

For example:

I make a commitment to find a new job or career that I will love within the next six months.

R is for Reality.

What is the current situation?

What actions have you taken so far?

What worked and what didn't?

What could get in your way?

Then list anything that could stop you achieving this goal. It could be a lack of focus, not being sure where to start, lack of time to search, fear, lack of self-belief.

Next look at your Options.

*What steps could you take to achieve this goal? Not what **will** you do but what **could** you do if you wanted to.*

List as many ideas as you can.

For example:

- Plan time for your job search.

- Use EFT to clear your fears or lack of belief.

- Create a CV.

- Send it to a friend to critique.

- Join relevant job sites and recruitment agencies.

- Set up email alerts for certain jobs.

- Look at the top 100 employers list.

- Send a message out on social media that you are looking for a new role.

- Contact companies that you would like to work for directly. Be different and send them a video or audio message.

- Go to job fairs.

- Check whether moving department or office is an option.

And the W is for Will. What WILL you do by when?

- I commit to finding an EFT script to help me clear my fear.

- I commit to creating my CV within the next week, so I can send it to my friend next Monday

- I commit to spending an hour twice a week joining job sites and uploading my CV. I will set a reminder on my phone to remind me to do this on Tuesday and Thursday after dinner.

- I will research and call four recruitment agencies by Friday.

- I will ask HR whether an internal move is an option by the end of the week.

- I will check and reset my career goals once a week on a Monday evening. I will put this in my diary so I don't forget.

Simple, isn't it? When you are planning the specific things

that you need to do to achieve a goal, then you need to make sure they are SMART.

Specific

Measurable

Achievable

Realistic / Relevant

Timely

Keep your specific actions in the short term, i.e. over the next 2-4 weeks. Any longer and you are likely to procrastinate!

Have them somewhere you can focus on them daily. Keep them in sight.

Use reminders on your phone and diary reminders. Often the biggest reason for failure to achieve goals is lack of focus.

If finding a new career is a goal for you, don't forget to create a Career playlist on the HappiMe app and listen as many times as you can.

Make a commitment to do at least one thing every single day to move you towards your goals. It doesn't have to be a huge thing. Consistency is key. The time will pass anyway and 365 actions, however small, will definitely bring you closer to success.

Living Life on Purpose

"I truly believe that everything that we do and everyone that we meet is put in our path for a purpose. There are no accidents; we're all teachers – if we're willing to pay attention

to the lessons we learn, trust our positive instincts and not be afraid to take risks or wait for some miracle to come knocking at our door." –Marla Gibbs

A question I get asked a lot is, "how do I find my passion or my purpose?" I have included some great questions below that may help you to understand your purpose or passion, but first I want to say a couple of key points:

1. Don't overcomplicate it. Some people spend so long "searching for their purpose" that they get frustrated and miss the point. Happiness is a state of mind, not a destination. You don't have to be "living your purpose" to be happy. In fact, I think that the happier you choose to be, and the more you decide to enjoy life, the easier it is to find your true calling. Your passion may be helping others, gardening, cooking, reading, writing, music or singing. For others, it may be volunteering, starting businesses, skydiving or travelling.

2. Decide each day that today will be a great day, and do as much as you can of the stuff that makes you feel good. Some of you will be lucky enough to make money doing the thing you love and some of you won't but will find huge fulfilment in following your passion in your spare time.

Questions to help you discover your life's purpose

- What makes you smile?

- When in your life have you felt truly happy?

- What makes the time fly by? What activities make you lose track of time?

- What makes you feel great about yourself?

- What inspires you?

- What makes you come alive?

- What are your strengths?

- What are your values?

- What are you naturally good at?

- What do you do effortlessly?

- What is your passion?

- What would you do if money was no object?

- What do people typically ask you to help them with?

- Where do you add the most significant value?

- How will you measure your life?

- What can I teach others?

- What do you like doing for others?

- How can you help others overcome challenges by telling them what you have overcome?

- How can you make a difference?

- How could your story help others?

- What do you want your friends to say about you at your funeral?

- If you were to die tomorrow, what would be your biggest regret?

- At the end of your life, after all, your accomplishments and actions are said and done, what will your Wikipedia entry read?

- What would you do with your life if you were guaranteed not to fail?

- When do you feel the most motivated?

- Why are you here?

- What do you dream about?

A Few Words About Your RAS

Your RAS is your reticular activating system. It does lots of important things, one of which is to act as a filter to the millions of pieces of data that are being thrown at us at any one time. If we go into a busy environment, there can be up to 2 million bits of data coming at us at any one time in the form of images, colours, sounds, emotions, tastes, and sensations.

Imagine your brain is like a computer – what would happen if you threw 2 million bits of data at a computer? It would freeze or blow up, right? So, the filter is a good thing. It blocks out most of this data and only lets stuff through the filter that it knows is important to us.

And how does it know that? By what we say and what we think.

Let me give you a couple of examples of your RAS in play...

Have you ever bought a new car, got it out onto the road and realised that every other car on the road is the same car? Or you start dating someone that drives a yellow car, and suddenly there are yellow cars everywhere? The cars were always there but your RAS was not set to notice them, so it filtered them out.

Another example is how we can go into a crowded room and quickly spot the one person we are looking for amongst hundreds. Our RAS filters out everybody else for us.

The last example is a personal one. About nine years ago I took on a loft conversion company as a business coaching client. Up until that stage in my life, loft conversions were not really on my radar. I didn't have one, I didn't want one, and didn't really know anyone who had one. I left the new client's office, and on the short 20-minute drive home I noticed two vans with loft conversions signs on the side and a scaffolding banner advertising a local loft conversion company. As I neared home, I noticed a huge loft conversion sign on the side of a building, one that had apparently been there for years, but I had never noticed it before. My RAS was now well and truly set on loft conversions!

Your RAS shows how crucial it is to be careful about what you say to yourself. If you wake up and tell yourself that today is going to be a bad day, your RAS is set and will spend the day letting things through your filter that back up what you have said.

So... you will notice that someone didn't put the top on the toothpaste. You will notice the driver that doesn't let you out at the junction. You will notice the person who didn't hold the door, and probably a hundred other things that will back up your belief that today is going to be a bad day.

On the flip side, by being aware of what you are saying to yourself, and changing the negative thought to a positive one (like, "today's going to be a great day"), you can completely turn your day around. Your RAS is now set to notice the positive stuff. So, you will notice that your clothes feel a little looser. You will notice the person that lets you out at the junction. Or the person that holds the door open for you.

Whether you think your day is going to be a good day or a bad day – either way you will be right.

Your RAS plays a vital part in goal-setting. When you write down your goals and set an intention to achieve them, your RAS will be on the lookout for things that can help you achieve them.

For example, I wrote on my 101 list that I wanted to go up in a hot air balloon. I told my friend Natalie that this was something I wanted to do, and two weeks later she called me to say that she had just read about a special offer for a balloon flight for two and would I like her to book it for us. Not only was my RAS set but so was hers!

Chapter in a nutshell

- Writing your goals down makes it far more likely that you will achieve them.

- Your RAS filter shows you more of what you focus on.

- Use the GROW model to self-coach: Goal, Reality, Options, Will.

- Make sure your short-term goals are SMART: Specific. Measurable, Achievable, Realistic, Timely.

Actions

- Write your 101 list.

- Set your RAS daily to look for the good things in life.

- Set SMART goals to help you achieve your goals.

- Coach yourself using the GROW model.

WHY WE DON'T ALWAYS ACHIEVE OUR GOALS

"Failure should be our teacher, not our undertaker. Failure is delay, not defeat. It is a temporary detour, not a dead end. Failure is something we can avoid only by saying nothing, doing nothing, and being nothing." –Denis Waitley

There are many reasons why we don't always achieve our goals, but I think they all pretty much boil down to the same thing:

What you believe to be true about yourself!

I am sure you have already got the message on this one, but just in case, I passionately believe that the number one reason you are not living your dream life is your belief system.

If your belief system is set to "I am not good enough, I'm not worth it, I'm a failure, or I never seem to get what I want", then you will never make long-term improvements to your life until you change that belief.

Here are a few others that link in...

Lack of clarity over what you want

Lack of clarity will often stem from a lack of self-belief. If you believe change is hard your chimp will put obstacles in your mind and find "reasons" why you shouldn't or can't.

Work on believing that change is possible. Rather than just telling yourself you don't know what you want (which closes your mind down), ask yourself some good open questions.

1. If I could wave a magic wand and change my life – what would be different?

2. If money was no object and I couldn't fail – what would I do?

Alternatively, simply asking "What don't I want?", can be a quick way to get started. Understanding what you don't want, can help you can clarify what you do want.

Lynn came to her first session knowing that she wanted something to be different but didn't know what she wanted to change so we started with the "So, what don't you want" approach. Looking at it this way enabled her to see things from a different perspective.

"I don't want to be unhappy anymore" was her initial reply. I asked her what made her unhappy. She thought for a moment and then said, "My job, when my husband and kids take me for granted, and my weight."

I asked her to rate each of these areas on a scale of one to ten – ten being intolerable. She replied:

The job is a 6/10 – it was bearable but needed to change.

Being taken for granted was a 9/10 – it was driving her nuts.

Her weight was 7/10 – was getting her down on a daily basis.

We delved deeper into what was happening at home, talked about how her husband and kids took her for granted and came up with a solid plan for how she was going to deal with it. She had a family meeting and told them that she needed their help around the house, she drew up a "rota" of tasks for the children and told her husband that any of his dirty clothes that didn't make it into the laundry basket, wouldn't make it into the washing machine either. It was interesting to see how fast he learned not to throw his dirty clothes on the floor!

By thinking about what she didn't want, Lynn was able to highlight the things that needed to change. Once things started to improve at home, she was able to spend more time on herself, especially around meal planning and exercise, which then helped her weight. Because she had stood up for herself at home, her confidence also started to improve at work. She asked her manager for more responsibility, which she was given. This meant that she was no longer unhappy at work either. Win-win-win. Just by thinking about what she didn't want.

Don't know where to start

Even thinking "I don't know where to start" is a belief that is not helping you. How about trying, "OK, if I did know where to start, what would I do?" or "If I could do one thing to move forward on this – what would it be?".

Or ask yourself what you would tell a friend who was thinking about doing the same thing? Often taking ourselves out of the picture makes it easier to gain clarity about what needs to be done.

Just list one thing you could do today that would bring you a little closer to achieving your goal. And then do it. Action has magic in it. You don't need to map out a detailed five-year plan before you move forward – you just need to know your first steps. And take them.

Lack of commitment

I am sure we have this one covered too. Lack of commitment is also often linked to your belief system – usually one or more of the following beliefs:

- I'm not good enough.

- I can't.

- Whatever I do always fails.

- Fear of success.

- Fear of failure.

- I'm not worth it.

Or perhaps the goal is not really your goal. Maybe it's a goal your spouse, parents or boss think you should achieve and you go along with it?

Commitment, like action, has magic in it. In the words of Napoleon Hill:

"The moment you commit and quit holding back, all sorts of unforeseen incidents, meetings, and material assistance, will rise up to help you. The simple act of commitment is a powerful magnet for help."

Not enough reasons why

If you skipped the exercise in the Leverage chapter, go and complete it now. Write a list of benefits for improving in the area you are focusing on. Write as many as you can. Ask yourself how important the goal is to you on a scale of one to ten. If it's not that important to you, then you may find your motivation slipping at the first obstacle. Make an absolute commitment to yourself that you will do what it takes.

Goals are too difficult

Break your goals down into bite-sized chunks. What is one thing you can do today to move you forward to your goals? Make a commitment to do at least one small thing every day to move you closer to your dream life.

Not managing your chimp

By now I am sure you understand the importance of noticing your chimp talk and are already taking steps to tell your chimp to back off!

Lack of time

This one is just an excuse. We all have the same number of hours in the day, and it never fails to amaze me how productive some people can be compared to others. It's just a matter of working as efficiently as possible and prioritising.

When asked if they had done any reading between sessions, my clients would often try the "I didn't have time" excuse. They only tried it once. My stock answer to this was, "If I offered you £10k to read that book within a week, would you have found the time?"

Of course, the answer was always yes! The reward was big enough to make it a top priority. If your goals are not taking precedence, then go back to your reasons why. Your rewards. Make them bigger and brighter. Or change the goal to something that does excite you. Look for ways to save time in other areas. Get up earlier. Stop watching TV. Stop trying to do everything for everyone else. And of course, there is also an element of discipline needed here. In the words of Nike – "Just do it".

Procrastination

Procrastination is the art of putting off tasks that you know you really should do today. Listening to your chimp is the most significant cause of procrastination, so tell him or her to back off.

Learn to "eat that frog". According to Brian Tracey, your "frog" is the thing you are most likely to procrastinate over. The thing on your to-do list that you really don't want to do. His advice is that if the worst thing you have to do that day is to eat a live frog, then for goodness sake eat it for breakfast rather than looking at it sat on the side of your plate all day. Every time you think of eating your frog or look at something on your to-do list that you don't want to do, it drains your energy a little. Get into the habit of doing these things first. Trust me; you will feel better for it.

Focusing on the wrong things

Being busy with stuff is often just another form of procrastination. Ask yourself every hour – is what I am doing right now the best use of my time? If it is not, then stop whatever you are doing and focus on the important stuff first.

Trying to change too many things at once

The more things you try to change at the same time, the less likely you are to succeed. Develop good habits in one area first.

Listening to the wrong people

Have you noticed that as soon as you talk about going into business or doing something different with your life, everyone's an expert?

Do not take financial advice from the bloke down the pub or your broke friend.

Do not take advice on how to be successful from unsuccessful people.

Do not take advice on how to be happy from unhappy people!

It sounds like common sense, but millions of people get talked out of their dreams by so-called experts every single day. My advice is to nurture your new goals and keep them close to your chest until you are strong enough to cope with everyone else's opinions. Although they would never admit to it, remember that some people don't want you to get on in life, for fear of you leaving them behind. This is a sad but true fact.

Guard your dreams fiercely and get around positive people whenever you can.

Read positive books or listen to positive audio every day. There are thousands of videos on YouTube that you can watch or listen to for free. Anything by Les Brown, Tony Robbins or Zig Ziglar would be a great start.

FEAR

You may have heard of the acronym for FEAR?

False Evidence Appearing Real

And yes, this is true, but fear of failure, fear of success, fear of rejection or fear of the unknown can be completely overwhelming, debilitating and feel very real. Your chimp is very powerful when he doesn't want to do something. He can make you wake up in the middle of the night in a cold sweat. He can cause endless anxiety and worry. Or he can stop you taking action and leave you feeling pretty disappointed in yourself.

Feel the Fear and Do It Anyway is a title of another great book by Susan Jeffers. The basic concept of the book is in the title. Understand that the thought of doing something is often far worse than the reality. Push yourself out of your comfort zone and see what happens. Just take some small steps to overcome the fear. I am sure there will be no broken bones, and not only will you have survived the experience but you will feel better about yourself because of it.

So, what else can you do about this besides understanding that your chimp is scared? You could try writing a **Worry List.** Write a list of everything you are worried about or fearful of. This it is a great exercise to do, just getting everything out of your head and onto paper is very therapeutic. Just seeing your fears and worries on paper can give you an entirely different perspective on them.

Next, go through your list and cross out the things that you have no influence over. Get rid of the things that you can do nothing about. Worrying about these things will be a complete and utter waste of time and energy.

Then create a **Wait to Worry List** and move anything that could be a problem in the future to this list. Then commit to only worrying about these things, if and when they actually become a real problem.

Most people find that most of the things on their worry list can be crossed off their list completely, or moved to their **Wait to Worry List**.

You may be left with a small list of worries and fears that you CAN influence. Decide to do something to improve the situation and take a small step to overcome the fear or solve the problem. Taking control and being proactive is hugely empowering. You've got this!

Chapter in a nutshell

The principal reasons for not achieving your goals are:

- What you believe to be true about yourself.

- Lack of clarity over what you want.

- Don't know where to start.

- Lack of commitment.

- Not enough reasons why.

- Goals are too difficult.

- Not managing your chimp.

- Lack of time. Procrastination.

- Focusing on the wrong things.

- Trying to change too many things at once.

- Listening to the wrong people.

- Allowing FEAR to take over.

Actions

- Understand what may get in your way and plan for it. Don't use any of the above as an excuse.

THE LAW OF ATTRACTION

"See the things that you want as already yours. Know that they will come to you at need. Then let them come. Don't fret and worry about them. Don't think about your lack of them. Think of them as yours, as belonging to you, as already in your possession". –Robert Collier

What is the Law of Attraction?

If you have never heard of the LOA then a) where have you been hiding? and b) please be prepared to get excited. I have been a passionate believer of the LOA for about 20 years and could literally bore you to tears with hundreds of stories where it has had a massive positive impact on my life.

Simply put, the Law of Attraction is the ability to attract into our lives whatever we are focusing on. "Like attracts like." It forms the basis for positive thinking but is much more than that.

The LAW of attraction means that you create your reality through the power of your thoughts and feelings. With your beliefs, thoughts, and actions, you energetically vibrate at a specific frequency, and the universe delivers circumstances, people and things into your life that vibrate or are aligned with that frequency.

For example, if you think predominately angry thoughts you will attract angry people and experiences into your life. If you continuously think about how fat you are, you will simply attract more of the same. The quickest way to attract more positive experiences in your life is to think and feel more positively about your life in general.

You are the "author" of your story. You decide what your life will be like. You decide whether it will be a happy, fulfilling one or a dreary, unhappy one by the thoughts and pictures you allow into your mind.

All the things you have learned so far will help you do that. The law of attraction is an amazing added bonus that kicks in when you are thinking positively about yourself, feeling gratitude, doing your affirmations and visualising your dream life. The universe always delivers. Sometimes it takes longer than you want and sometimes it can happen so quickly that it will blow your socks off!

Everything is universal energy

The chair that you are sat on, the clothes you are wearing, your house, your car, plants, trees, and flowers. EVERYTHING and that includes YOU. This is something the world of quantum physics has known for years. It's a proven, scientific fact.

Energy follows thought

Our thoughts and feelings send out a vibration, and universal energy matches our vibration by giving us more of the same.

Utilizing the Law of Attraction for your benefit is about finding the frequency of your desire by adopting a self-love practice, acting as if you're already living the life you want, visualising your ideal situation, affirming what you want instead of what is, and finding ways to feel now how you would feel then.

What you focus on you get more of...

- Like attracts like.

- You become what you think about.

- What you think about you bring about.

- If you think you can, you can!

- If you think you can't, you can't!

- Your thoughts shape your reality.

- You reap what you sow.

- What goes around comes around.

- What you put out there you get back.

Sound too good to be true? Maybe, but what if it is true? What have you got to lose by testing out the LOA? Nothing! You could, on the other hand, gain an awful lot.

You are where you are right now because of your past thoughts, beliefs and actions. The LOA is already working for all of us, all of the time, so it makes sense to use it to help you to achieve your dream life rather than not actively using it and potentially sabotaging yourself.

Key points to remember

The LOA won't work if...

- You just expect to sit on a mountain visualising that a Ferrari will suddenly appear on your drive.

- You say positive affirmations for 10 minutes a day and

then are negative for the rest of the day.

- You just write a list of your goals like a shopping list without evoking feelings and emotions.

- You don't tackle the self-sabotaging beliefs that are stopping you from achieving your goals.

- Your goals are sat in a notepad or a drawer, never seeing the light of day.

- You don't visualise yourself succeeding EVERY DAY.

- You talk or think consistently about what you don't want.

- You fret about it not working or worry about the how, when and where.

But it will work if ...

- You get off your backside and take inspired action!

- Your number one focus each day is feeling good and feeling positive. Repeatedly tell yourself that your life is good and getting better.

- You are grateful for what you already have in your life. (More on that later.)

- You get in control of your thoughts and only think about what you do want.

- You set an intention. You clarify your goals. What are you looking to achieve and by when? How will achieving these goals make you feel? More confident? Happier?

- You imagine, with as much feeling and emotion as you can, that you have ALREADY achieved those goals. You visualise your ideal life daily, go off to sleep feeling how great you feel as you have already achieved success. Image with as much emotion as you can how you will feel, how will you look, what you will be wearing and what you want to be doing. More on visualising in the next chapter.

- You do a vision board. Get pictures of your goals and pin them all over the house! Or create a Goals & Intentions book and carry it with you. Put pictures of your goals on your screensaver on your laptop and mobile.

- You use EFT to tackle those deep-rooted beliefs once and for all.

- You let go and trust that the universe will deliver. Trust that the universe has your back. Don't doubt because when you doubt you block what you are trying to manifest. If you go back to your old way of thinking – you will go back to your old life. It's that simple.

- You are aware of the inspired nudges the universe is sending you.

Here are just a few things that I have manifested into my life using the LOA:

Easy weight loss.

By visualising daily, my belief in myself to lose weight and keep it off got stronger and stronger until there was absolutely no doubt in my mind that I was going to crack it once and for all. One of my daily mantras was "this is really easy", and funnily enough, it was!

Regular perfect parking spaces.

One of the easiest ways that you can test the universe and the LOA is to always visualise parking in the precise spot you want. I dare you to try it. As you are driving towards your destination, see yourself pulling into the perfect spot. I do this everywhere I go and always get the ideal spot. Whenever I meet my friends for a coffee or lunch they always laugh to see my car is always parked right outside the restaurant!

An amazing business.

As I mentioned in Chapter One, my business coaching practice literally came at me from three different directions just hours after I put out an intention.

Too many holidays and trips to mention.

For the last five years, each time I have wanted a holiday, I have simply put an intention out to the universe to attract the amount of money I needed for the trip. And every time, within two weeks (and sometimes a lot quicker) I have been sent enough new business to pay for the trips! A month in Bali, two weeks in Mexico, two weeks with Tony Robbins in New York, Greece (twice), Gran Canaria for Christmas, Lanzarote, Thailand and Spain six times! I kid you not.

A £45k Car

We talked about SMART goals in the previous chapter (Specific, Measurable, Achievable, Realistic and Timed). Yes, I believe that smart goals are perfect when it comes to the day to day actions that you need to take, but I believe when it comes to longer-term goals, SMART goals can stop you from dreaming big. I had a picture of a Mercedes E Class Convertible on my screensaver for ten years before I was able to buy one. When I put the picture on my computer, I had no idea of when or how I was going to get it, I just trusted that if I worked smart enough, one day I would have it. And I did. A brand new one. If I had allowed myself to get caught up in the how that car may have never made it to my goals list.

Those of you that are new to the LOA may well be thinking that I am stark raving bonkers at this point. But please don't take my word for it. Go and research it yourself. Try it – especially the "perfect parking space". There are hundreds of millions of people out there who believe in the LOA, including famous people like Will Smith, Oprah, Jim Carrey, Kanye West, Arnold Schwarzenegger, Jay Z, Andrew Carnegie, Denzel Washington, Lady Gaga, LMFAO and Steve Harvey, just to name a few. What have you got to lose?

"All that we are is a result of what we have thought." –Buddha

Chapter in a nutshell

- What you think about you bring about. Like energy attracts like energy.

- Manifesting with the LOA is all about feelings and emotions, not lists of goals. Ask for it, see yourself achieving it with as much feeling as you can, imagine as if it is already here and let it go to receive it.

Actions

- Focus only on what you want.

- Let go of any attachment.

- If you don't get what you want, assume that something better is on its way.

- Be patient.

- If you are new to the LOA, watch *The Secret* on YouTube (search *The Secret, full movie*).

- Read *The Magic* by Rhonda Byrne.

THE PHENOMENAL POWER OF VISUALISATION

"Visualise this thing that you want, see it, feel it, believe in it. Make your mental blueprint, and begin to build." –Robert Collier

So, let's talk about the fantastic power of visualisation and clarify exactly what visualisation is.

Visualisation, also known as Visual Mental Rehearsal, is the process of imagining events or objects in your mind's eye in order to achieve a desired outcome.

Most people can visualise. Let me give you an example – what colour is your door?

When you thought about that question, you would have mentally brought up an image of your door and what it looks like, to identify the colour. That is visualisation. Some people get full HD colour images, and some get vague images. Either is good. If you are one of the very few people who simply can't visualise, don't panic – just go with the feeling of having what you want, rather than seeing the actual images.

I believe that learning to visualise is a skill you can learn, just like any other skill. As with any new skill, practice helps. Visualisation techniques can be strengthened when you start to make the images brighter and stronger, adding colour, movement, smell, sounds and most importantly – emotion.

Many influential people, athletes, and celebrities have discovered the amazing power of visualisation, and have used it to achieve the life of their dreams. Positive visualisation is fun, exciting and very empowering.

Numerous studies have proven that the brain does not know the difference between imagining something or doing it. Therefore, visualising positive outcomes enables both the brain and the body to become responsive and conditioned to that result. In other words, we are kidding our subconscious mind into believing that something is happening in the way we want it to happen.

In a famous study that appeared an important psychology journal a few years ago (*North American Journal of Psychology*), athletes who mentally practised a hip-flexor exercise had strength gains that were almost as significant as those in people who did the exercise five times a week for 15 minutes on a weight machine. How amazing is that?

Many sports people and celebrities have used mental imagery and visualisation to increase their success for years.

Tiger Woods started using visualisation techniques from a very early age. He has been using the incredible power of his mind to form images and visualise exactly where he wants his golf ball to stop for years. He is now one of the most famous and successful golf players in the world.

Another great example is the famous Hollywood star and governor of California, Arnold Schwarzenegger. He has used visualisation techniques to fulfil his hopes and dreams from a very young age. When he first started out as a bodybuilder, he used to visualise what it would be like to win the title of Mr Universe, and then he acted as if he had already won it, which he did a few years later.

Perhaps one of the most famous people in the world who openly uses visualisation techniques is Oprah Winfrey. She often talks about the power of the subconscious mind, affirmations and other goal focusing techniques on her talk show.

And there are many others such as such as Anthony Robbins and Bill Gates, who all have claimed that visualisation has played a significant role in their success.

Visualisation is about taking your personal improvements to the next level by creating a short movie in your mind where you have already achieved what you are affirming. You can have one movie that incorporates all your goals, or you can have a different movie for each – it is entirely up to you.

Personally, I tend to create movies that encompass all that I am looking to achieve as I find that much more fun and exciting.

Here are my Top tips for Visualising a Great Movie in your Mind:

1. When you first start, it's easier if you write your visualisation down. Think about exactly what you want to visualise. What does happiness/confidence/success look like? What do you want to achieve? What will you be doing?

The easiest way to do this is to write out your movie scenes by listing them as simple bullet points.

For example, if your goal is to be more confident:

• Scene 1: See yourself in your favourite outfit looking

fantastic and feeling confident.

- Scene 2: Imagine listening to what your friends are saying about how confident you are.

- Scene 3: See yourself doing the things you want to be more confident at.

Make sense?

2. Think about success as if it has ALREADY happened. Your subconscious mind cannot take an instruction for the future. It can only work in the present. This is one of the most important things to remember when creating your visualisation movie. It must be in the present tense as if it has already happened. Not in the future, or that is where it will stay.

3. The second most important thing to remember is that you want to think about how you will FEEL doing these things. Think about success as if it has ALREADY happened. Really feel the excitement, confidence and happiness.

(There is a brilliant audio on the HappiMe app called Confident Me which will take you through the process of relaxing and visualising yourself feeling confident.)

4. Don't try too hard or over-complicate things. As I said, not everyone can visualise full blown, 30-minute, HD colour movies. Brief, vague images or feelings are totally fine – your subconscious mind will still get the picture.

5. Another thing to remember is that your mind doesn't have to be completely clear for you to relax and visualise. In fact, when you first start you will probably find loads of random thoughts popping into your head. That's OK. Just let them

come and go, don't focus on them, just focus on your breath. Again... the more you practise, the easier it will get.

6. Remember that you are already great at visualising. Only now you are probably visualising negative things happening to you. That's what you are doing when you are worrying about something. You are imagining all the terrible things that could go wrong. That's visualising.

7. Understand that when you repeatedly imagine performing a task, you also condition your neural pathways so that the action feels familiar when you go to perform it; it's as if you're carving a groove in your brain, like the groove on a record.

Just in case you didn't get the message...

Imagining success as it has already happened and with the same emotions as you will feel when you achieve success, are the two most important things you can do. Simply seeing the pictures in your mind is not enough – you must show your brain which feelings it must look out for.

Envelop yourself in these wonderful positive emotions. Experience exactly what you would experience if your dreams had come true. You will no doubt feel joy, pride, success, happiness, wealth, and confidence...

8. Practise your visualisation as often as you can. While you are waiting for the kettle to boil, while you are cleaning your teeth, before you go off to sleep, as soon as you wake up in the morning, whenever you are bored! The more you do it, the quicker you'll reprogramme your mind and the easier it will be when you come to do it.

Other Great Tools to Help with Visualisation

- Create your dream or vision board.

- Print pictures of the goals from your 101 list and create a collage of your goals and dreams.

- Write your top goals down every day.

- Get yourself a goal book and write your goals out, over and over – again – write them as if you have already achieved them.

Write me a letter

Write a letter to me, as if it was one year from now. Write the letter as if the year has already passed and you are telling me about all the great positive changes you have made and the wonderful experiences you are having in your life.

Start with "Hey Jo. You are not going to believe what amazing things are going on in my life!", and then tell me about them as if they have already happened. Use as many positive descriptive words as you can like wonderful, amazing, exciting, passionate, loving, delightful and fantastic.

Keep your letter by your bedside (or on your phone if it's private) and read it before you go to bed and when you get up in the morning. Read it with as much excitement as you can!

Pretend Conversations

This one is great for when you are driving, especially if you are on a long drive and feeling a little sleepy, as it will energise you quicker than a strong coffee. Simply pretend you are calling me to tell me about all the wonderful things that have happened – exactly like in your letter. Be excited and have some fun with it. Nobody is listening – unless you are in a soft top at the traffic lights of course, and then (hopefully) you will just look like you are on the phone!

Does it sound a little mad? Yes, probably, but it works, so I challenge you to try it – it's great fun (although if you do it in the car, please make sure you are paying attention to the roads!).

Good luck with your visualisation, letters and pretend conversations. I promise you are going to be energised, excited and intoxicated with the unbeatable feeling of achievement.

Chapter in a nutshell

- Visualisation, also known as Visual Mental Rehearsal, is the process of imagining events or objects in your mind's eye in order to achieve a desired outcome.

- Numerous studies have proven that the brain does not know the difference between imagining something or doing it.

- Many sports people and celebrities have used mental imagery and visualisation to increase their success for years.

- When you first start, it's easier if you write your visualisation down.

- Think about success as if it has ALREADY happened and think about how you will FEEL doing these things. Envelop yourself in these wonderful positive emotions. Experience exactly what you would experience if your dreams had come true.

Actions

- Create your dream or vision board.

- Write your top goals down every day.

- Write me a letter and record your letter on the HappiMe app.

- Have fun pretend conversations.

- Listen to Confident Me on the HappiMe app.

- Practise your visualisation as often as you can.

THE ASTONISHING POWER OF GRATITUDE

"I don't have to chase extraordinary moments to find happiness – it's right in front of me if I'm paying attention and practising gratitude." – Brene Brown

It's a fact – keeping a gratitude journal makes you happier.

Practicing gratitude for five minutes a day has been proven to increase your long-term happiness and wellbeing by more than 10%, which is about the same impact as doubling your income. Assuming that most people are unlikely to double their income over the next six months, I would most definitely recommend practising gratitude as an alternative way of bringing more happiness into your life. It also just happens to be the easiest and fastest way to feel more positive and optimistic.

There are a couple of excellent reasons for this…

Firstly, you are setting your RAS to notice the good things in your life, so this smart little filter will let more "good things" through for you to notice and be grateful for.

And secondly, the more you focus on what's great in your life, with passion and emotion, the higher your vibrations are. The higher your vibrations are – the more amazing synchronicities will unfold, and fantastic manifestations will appear.

Now, as already discussed, some of you may be thinking that this all sounds a little bit too good to be true. If that's you, I challenge you to practise gratitude for the next month and just watch what happens in your life. What have you got to lose? Nothing. But on the other hand, you could have a tremendous amount to gain. In fact, it could be life-changing for you.

There have been hundreds of studies showing the fabulous benefits of gratitude. Just in case you are not convinced, here are another ten marvellous reasons to give thanks for what is good in your life.

1. You live longer

Being grateful leads you to become more optimistic. And optimism has been shown to increase our longevity according to the University of Kentucky.

2. Improves your career

Gratitude makes you a more effective employee. It makes networking easier, increases your decision-making capabilities, increases your productivity, and helps you attract mentors. As a result, gratitude helps you achieve your career goals, as well as making your workplace a more friendly and enjoyable place to be.

3. Increases your likability

Manchester University found that gratitude generates social capital. Studies showed that people who were 10% more grateful than average had 17.5% more social capital. Gratitude helps you to make friends and deepens existing friendships and relationships.

4. Improves your sleep

According to a study conducted by the University of California, your sleep quality improves by 25% and you get 8% more sleep.

5. Reduces depression

Keeping a gratitude journal reduces depression by 30%+ for as long as the practice continues (2005 Positive Psychology progress).

6. You will exercise more

Practising gratitude results in up to 19% increase in time spent exercising.

7. Gives you pain relief

10% of those studied also reported a 10% reduction in physical pain.

8. Helps you bounce back quicker

Those who have more gratitude have a more proactive coping style, are more likely to have and seek out social support in times of need, are less likely to develop PTSD, and are more likely to grow in times of stress.

9. Helps you relax

Gratitude and positive emotion, in general, are among the strongest relaxants known.

10. You'll feel good

According to gratitude researcher Robert Emmons, gratitude is just happiness that we recognise after the fact, to have been caused by the kindness of others. Gratitude doesn't just make us happier; it is happiness in and of itself!

Hopefully, I have persuaded you to at least try practising gratitude as a way of being happier?

So... what are the various ways to practise gratitude?

Give thanks in the moment

This one goes hand in hand with practising mindfulness. Just stop, notice and give thanks.

Here are a few of mine to get you started:

- Pause long enough to appreciate a beautiful flower or plant, a sunset or sunrise, the sound of the wind in the trees or how wonderful the sun feels on your face.

- Acknowledge nice people and good service.

- Savour tasty food, enjoy bubble baths and comfortable beds.

- Give thanks that the traffic lights are on your side, for the perfect parking spaces, your car flying through its MOT.

Keep a gratitude journal

So, what's a gratitude journal and what should you write in it?

Any of the above for starters. Go back over your day and think about all the good things that have happened. Some days will be easier than others no doubt. Here are a few of mine from the last couple of weeks:

- A healthy body

- Cupcakes on my son's birthday

- Lunch with my lovely sister and her husband

- Enjoying going to the movies with my kids

- A fantastic new vegan recipe site

- Clearing the attic with my son

- Technology, especially my iPhone

- Egyptian cotton sheets

- My thirst for knowledge

- The fact that I can work from home and set my own hours

- Grey's Anatomy

- My Dad

- My fabulous car

- Meditating in the sunshine

- Cashew vegan garlic cheese

- Maintaining my weight loss

- Game of Thrones

- My wealth and abundance

- A fantastic new business coaching client

Ideally, write 3-5 things each day – different if you can.

Gratitude stone or pebble

Many people have a special gratitude pebble or stone that they keep in their pocket as a reminder to give thanks.

Gratitude habits

I have been practising gratitude for years, so I don't always write things down now as I have developed a habit of gratitude. I am grateful in the moment, and I tend to think about the things I am grateful for as I am cleaning my teeth before bedtime. The easiest way to create a habit is to hook it onto another, already established habit, like cleaning your teeth.

Chapter in a nutshell

- It's a fact – keeping a gratitude journal makes you happier.

- You are setting your RAS to notice the good things in your life.

- The more you focus on what's great in your life, with passion and emotion, the higher your vibrations are. The higher your vibrations are – the more amazing synchronicities will unfold, and fantastic manifestations will appear.

Key benefits of gratitude:

- You will live longer, improves your career, increases your likability. Improve your sleep, reduces depression. You will exercise more, bounce back quicker, relax more and you'll feel happier. Why on earth wouldn't you try it if it can give you all this?!

Actions

- Give thanks in the moment

- Keep a gratitude journal

- Have a gratitude stone or pebble

- Create gratitude habits

STRATEGIES FOR HAPPINESS

"Success is not the key to happiness. Happiness is the key to success. If you love what you are doing, you will be successful."
–Albert Schweitzer

I hope that this chapter will give you some inspiration as to some of the simple happiness strategies that you can adopt to ensure that you live a happy and fulfilling life.

Recognising when your chimp is running the show will be a tremendous help when it comes to taking up new hobbies, making new friends and having wonderful new experiences. When your chimp panics or encourages you to procrastinate, you now have powerful techniques like EFT, CBT, NLP and mindfulness to calm him down.

The most important strategies we have already covered fully in previous chapters, so I have simply listed them here. I consider the first seven essential to long-term happiness:

- Recognise your chimp talk and learn to choose more helpful thoughts.

- Choose your attitude daily. Don't look for happiness – create it. Decide to be happy. Come from a place of love, not fear.

- Take responsibility for where you are right now and clear your stuff with tapping.

- Dream a little. Create your 101-bucket list. Visualise yourself happy and confident.

- Practise mindfulness or meditation daily.

- Write a gratitude list every day.

- Use the HappiMe app to help you do all of the above.

Get around positive, like-minded people.

Either in groups, on a one to one or online. Meetup is a brilliant resource to find like-minded people all around the world. Go to www.meetup.com and simply enter your hobbies and interests and it will show you groups of people all around you that like to do the same kind of things.

Or start your own group. I set up Positive People in Bristol just over a year ago, and we now have over 1,050 members.

Or search *personal development group your city* and see what comes up. You will be surprised how many positive people there are around.

Grow. Listen, watch or read inspirational and motivational stuff every day.

Most of the best books are on audio now, so you can download them onto your phone and listen at the gym, while you are in the car or out walking. Go to www.audible.com.

Watch on YouTube:

- Les Brown

- Tony Robbins

- Zig Ziglar

- Oprah

- Nick Vujicic

- *The Secret*, Abraham

- Wayne Dyer

Read:

- *Notes from the Universe* – daily email from TUT.com

- *The Chimp Paradox* (highly recommended)

- *Attitude is Everything* by Jeff Keller

- *Being Happy* by Andrew Matthews

- *Happy for No Reason* by Marci Shimoff

- *The Success Principles* by Jack Canfield

- *Think and Grow Rich* by Napoleon Hill

- *The Power of Now* by Eckhart Tolle

- *The Secret* and *The Magic* by Rhona Bryne

- *How to Win Friends and Influence People* by Dale Carnegie

- *Wishes Fulfilled* by Wayne Dyer

Listen:

1. *The Goals Program* by Zig Ziglar (great fun, highly recommended)

2. *Change Your Thoughts, Change Your Life* by Wayne Dyer

3. *Maximum Confidence* by Jack Canfield

4.   *Mindset* by Carole Dweck

5.   *Follow Your Passion, Find Your Purpose* by Bob Doyle

6.   Podcasts – there are millions of free podcasts available on just about every subject going.

Protect your positive energy.

Avoid negative media and movies with destructive content. Stop watching the news. Bad news sells which is why 90% of the news is usually negative. Seriously, I haven't watched the news in over 25 years. I still know what is going on in the world from skimming the BBC news app or someone will post about in on FB.

Clear your Facebook feed of all the moaners and whingers. You don't need to unfriend them – just unfollow them. Fill your newsfeed with positive quotes and videos.

Avoid the drains and mood hoovers. We all know them – the kind of person that you daren't ask how they are doing, as you know they will bore you to tears for the next hour, telling you about all their aches, pains and woes. Sometimes as we grow and develop, we leave some friends behind.

Listen to uplifting music, watch funny films, read inspirational stories.

Stop comparing yourself to others.

There is nothing to be gained by comparing yourself to others. In fact, it's one of the quickest routes to unhappiness. Social media has a lot to answer for on this one. We seem to have this obsession over creating a picture-perfect life. We see Facebook posts of our perfect friends having so much more fun that we are. They are partying, travelling, skiing, mountain climbing, baking the best cakes, receiving the most beautiful flowers, eating at the most romantic restaurants, wearing the best clothes while being forever in love with their soul-mate. Excuse me while I go throw up. It's all crap. It's fake. It's not real life. Those pictures are a tiny snippet in time.

People only tend to put things on social media that they want to you see. They don't want you to see the arguments, the loneliness, the anxiety or the tears, so they don't post about that. Oh no. Goodness, we can't have people seeing that kind of thing.

So, rather than thinking how much smarter, wealthier, or more attractive others are, enjoy and appreciate yourself. In the entire universe, there is no one quite like you. In fact, according to Mel Robbins, the likelihood of you being born **as you,** has been calculated at 1 in 400 trillion.

The world needs your authenticity and special skills.

Include an act of kindness in your life each day.

- Thank the people who serve you in the community. The shopkeeper, the bus drivers, etc.

- Give your seat up on the bus or subway.

- Pay it forward with a coffee.

- Give someone flowers because you can.

- Volunteer for organisations that help others.

- Bake someone a cake or invite someone over for dinner.

- Buy a homeless person a sandwich.

- Compliment someone on their parking skills.

- Send thank you cards.

Nurture your relationships.

If you just found out that you only had 24 hours left to live, who would you call and what would you tell them? Don't wait to be told that you only have 24 hours to live. Call them now. I wish I had called my Mum every day and told her that I loved her.

Do something thoughtful for your friends or family. Dedicate time to them. Plan a date night, mate night or kid's night in your diary if you have to.

Pick a relationship in need of strengthening, and invest time and energy in healing, cultivating, affirming and enjoying it.

Remember to compliment your friends and family when they look good.

Call or text your friends and family and tell them how grateful you are to have them in your life.

Write a card to someone you haven't seen in a while and tell them something nice.

Try to take note when people do a good job and give recognition when it's due at work.

Reward effort, if someone does something nice for you, do something nice for them.

Change your vocabulary.

Change "have to" to "get to".

Shifting your mindset from "I have to" to "I get to" is life-changing. The way we approach tasks plays a huge part in how motivated we are to do them.

*It's Friday evening, and Tina **has to go** grocery shopping.*

She's in a bad mood because she has to go shopping and would rather be at home with the kids. She moans to herself all the way around the store, resentful that she has to do this on a Friday night. Her bad mood means that she radiates negative energy, and she attracts more things to moan about. She gets hit on her ankles by a trolley, she can't find her favourite items, she misses the special offers as she is whizzing around, and the massive queues at the till are the last straw.

She couldn't wait to get out of there and get home. She arrives home in an even worse mood and spends the evening snapping at the kids.

*It's Friday evening, and Susan **gets to go** grocery shopping.*

She's in a good mood because she looks at her shopping time as a little "me" time.

She has made a list, so she knows it won't take long, and then she can be back home, to spend the night watching a movie with the kids.

She hums to herself all the way around, happy that she gets this time to herself to browse around the store.

Her good mood means she radiates positive energy and she attracts more things to feel good about.

She notices how friendly everyone is today, especially the lovely assistant who helped her find her favourite items. She chatted with her as they searched for her items. She spots some great special offers as she walks around including 2 for 1 on popcorn. The assistant walked with her towards the tills, and when she notices the queues, she ushered Susan to the end till, where she jumped on to serve her.

Susan arrives home in an even better mood and spends the evening watching movies and eating popcorn with the kids.

A rather cheesy example I know, but that tiny change of word can have an enormous impact on how you approach things.

Every time you hear yourself say "have to", change it quickly to "get to" and see how your mindset changes towards the task.

As you are learning, how we speak, both to ourselves and to others, has a tremendous impact on our mood and happiness. If someone asks how you are, and you answer, "I'm okay", or "I'm fine", then you will feel just that – fine, okay, neutral, apathetic.

But if you answer, "I'm great!" or "I'm feeling amazing today!" or "I'm really excited for my day," then you will feel excited, passionate and optimistic. The other person will look at you as if you are on drugs but who cares. I once read a book called *Better than Good* by Zig Ziglar, that suggested that whenever anyone asks you how you are, try saying "Actually, I'm better than good". Try it – it's brilliant, people do a double take and ask you why are you feeling so good. It's a great conversation starter.

Interestingly, changing your vocabulary can change your

emotional states even if you don't believe at first what we are saying. Next time you're angry, try saying to yourself, "I'm a little annoyed" instead of "I'm furious", and see how, by just lowering the emotional intensity of your words, you can create internal changes.

Find your flow.

Identify one or two activities that excite you, that challenge you, that makes you lose track of time when you're doing them. And then prioritise them. Don't just put them into the "when I have time then I'll do it" category. Make these times when you have "flow" in your life a regular part of your day because they will naturally infuse joy and energy into other areas of your life.

When I was recovering from chemo, I had plenty of time to think about my flow. What was I doing when time sped by fastest? What was I doing when I was enjoying every second of every minute? When did I feel most inspired and motivated? For me, it is when I am either coaching, public speaking or creating stuff that makes a difference. I committed to find time every day to do one of these things.

Aim to find a mix of activities that give you joy and a sense of meaning. A feeling of purpose increases your happiness levels. Some of you will be lucky enough to find a way to make a living from your passion, and some of you will find it in your hobbies.

Think about volunteer work or taking a cooking class. The positive feelings that come from these sorts of activities can help train the brain's neurons to overcome its negativity bias. As neuropsychologist Rick Hanson, Ph.D., explains in his book *Hardwiring Happiness*, the brain is all too good at remembering adverse experiences, which he traces to ancestors who had to focus on threats like predators in order to survive. But when you rack up feel-good experiences that give you a sense of achievement, they can serve as a buffer against the disappointing ones.

Search for meaning.

The happiest people find purpose in everything that they do. Their accomplishments aren't necessarily more significant than those of their less happy counterparts, but they personally find meaning in their work and their relationships. Keep searching for lessons in daily life. Find the meaning embedded in every experience.

Know your own bliss.

When was the last time you mulled over what truly brings you pleasure, aside from biggies like your partner and the kids?

Plan and prioritise.

What do you think are the top excuses that I hear from clients who haven't yet achieved the life of their dreams?

- I haven't got the time.

- I didn't have the time.

- I was too busy.

- Otherwise translated as...

- I didn't think I could do it.

- I didn't think it was important enough to find the time.

My stock answer to this is always the same.

If I said I would give you £10,000 to do "that" by next week – would you do it?

What do you think their answer would be? Always a *"yes, of course I would"*. It's funny how our priorities can change and time can appear from nowhere when the motivation is big enough.

Planning, organisation and prioritising is not everyone's strong point, so I thought it was crucial to include a section on it. I am going to introduce you to the simplest time management system ever – one that has worked for hundreds of clients, even those who were undeniably terrible at time management!

Buy an A4 ring-bound pad. This is important as you will be tearing a page out each day.

Project page: On the left-hand page, write headings for the key areas of your life, including any projects you are working on. I use the same one for work and home stuff. For example:

- Kids

- Home & Finances

- Health

- Work project 1

Under each heading, write everything you need to do. Break large projects down into bullet points for now; you don't need to go into loads of details.

Kids	House	Health	Work project 1
Buy trainers	Housework	Plan gym days	Arrange meeting
Sew trousers	Fix light	Plan meals	Set agenda
Organise party	Mow lawn	Order supplements	Organise slides
	Call bank	Book dentist	Email attendees
	Sort loan	Mindfulness	Order refreshments

On the right-hand side of the page, write the date at the top and then split the page into the following four quadrants. Do this at the END of the day – ready for the next day.

Urgent	Important
In here, write everything that MUST be done that day. Break the bigger tasks into bite-sized chunks.	Here you put the things that it would be nice to get done.
General	**Waiting for / don't forget**
Use this space for things that come up during the day. (shopping, calls).	Use this space to remind you of things that you are waiting for from others, that you need to be able to move forward. If this list gets too

	big, move it to the left-hand *projects* page.

Key tips

- Keep your Planning book somewhere where you can see it every day.

- Start straight on your urgent tasks. Don't look at your important for now until your urgent list is complete.

- As you achieve each task, either tick it off, cross it off or highlight it. This will release a shot of dopamine, the feel-good chemical, into your bloodstream, helping you to feel more motivated to achieve.

- Then at the end of each day, tear out your page, check your projects page and re-prioritise your urgent and important tasks.

It is a really simple process, and I promise that within a few weeks of using this system you will feel in control and proactive rather than overwhelmed and reactive.

Actions from this chapter

- Download the Happiness Strategies mind map from www.jorichings.com/whoops, print and stick it where you can see it.

30-DAY CHALLENGE!

30 Days to a Happier You!

Okay, we are nearly at the end of the book, so I thought a good way to finish up would be to pull all the key actions together and set you a 30-day challenge.

If you choose to commit to this 30-day challenge, I absolutely guarantee that it will be life-changing for you. Not only will you become aware of your own negative self-talk, but you will also start to notice how negative everyone else is around you. Getting in control of your thinking and becoming the master of your own mind is liberating and empowering. Your belief in yourself will improve. You will start to believe that things you once thought impossible are achievable. You will feel better each day, you will worry less and you will feel happier. You will be less anxious and spend more time in the moment rather than worrying about the past or future.

On the other hand, if you choose to "have a go" at this challenge, I can absolutely guarantee that this will not change your life in any way!

Commitment has magic in it.

The Six Steps to a Happier You…

So, here's the challenge. Over the next 30 days:

1. **Be super vigilant with your thoughts. Your**

happiness depends on it!

- Turn up the volume on your thoughts. Listen closely, recognise your unhelpful thoughts, and stamp on your ANTs (automatic negative thoughts).

2. **Interrupt the pattern.**

   - Delete, delete, distract yourself and challenge your thoughts.

3. **Replace the unhelpful thought with a slightly more helpful one.**

   - Create a playlist of your helpful thoughts on the HappiMe app and listen daily.

   - Write your helpful thoughts down every day

4. **Get out of your thinking mind.**

   - Learn to stay more present by practising a different mindfulness exercise every day.

5. **Practice Gratitude.**

   - For the next 30 days, as you go to sleep each night, write down 3-5 things you are grateful for, then really *feel* the gratitude, and then visualise yourself feeling happier and achieving your goals.

6. **Do something nice for yourself or others every day.**

Let's be fair, none of this is rocket science, is it? Being happier just takes a little focus sometimes. It's easy to focus on the wrong stuff but now you understand that focusing on the wrong stuff does not help you in any way, in fact, it hinders you by bringing more of what you don't want.

In her brilliant book *Happy for No Reason*, Marci Shimoff says that we each have a happiness "set point". We can have highs or lows but we always come back to the same "set point" afterwards.

By focusing on the Six Steps to a Happier You for 30 days, you will actually increase your happiness set point. You will still have your highs and lows and the bottom may very well drop out of your world again. That's life I'm afraid, but you'll find that you bounce back quicker. That outside influences do not affect you as much. That you'll feel happier and more in control.

I will repeat the sentiment that Randy Gage voiced at the seminar I attended – the one that turned out to be the catalyst to the end of my marriage...

There are three types of people reading this book along with you right now.

1. There are those of you that have promised yourselves that you will go back and do the exercises, and of course, will definitely do the 30-day challenge when you have more time. But you won't. Life will carry on as usual, and not much will change long-term.

2. There are those of you that have done some of the exercises and will start enthusiastically start the 30-day challenge, only to be distracted by life within a few weeks or even a few days. Some things may

change for you and you may feel better equipped to deal with the "Whoops" when they come along.

3. And there are those of that have done some or even all of the exercises and will commit to the 30-day challenge. You'll review the mind map daily, and you will share these technique with your loved ones.

Now, guess which group will go on to live happier, more relaxed and more fulfilled lives?

So lovely reader – which group do you want to be in?

I hope you are in the third group!

Actions from this Chapter

- Do the 30-day challenge. No really... **DO THE CHALLENGE!!!**
- And download the 30-day tracker to help you keep you on track at www.jorichings.com/whoops

EPILOGUE

So here we are at the end of the book already.

I sincerely hope that you have enjoyed reading it as much as I enjoyed writing it. And most importantly, that my words have inspired you to make positive changes in your own life. None of what I have written is rocket science. I am sure most of it seems like common sense to you. The magic is not in just knowing this stuff. You need to internalise and action what you have learned. Then the magic happens. I have watched thousands of people become happier, healthier and wealthier using these strategies and techniques.

What you have read in Part Two of this book (particularly in the last chapter) are the exact techniques that have enabled me to:

- Stay positive and motivated despite numerous curveballs.

- Go from being an unhappy, stressed, obese, workaholic who never exercised, to being happy, relaxed, fit and 100 pounds lighter.

- Build a very prosperous and abundant career in as a Business Coach & Happiness Coach, Author and Inspirational Speaker.

- Become a successful Social Entrepreneur creating tools, programmes and apps that make a positive difference in the world, including HappiMe, an innovative app aimed at raising self-esteem and happiness levels in children, young people, and adults.

- Create a level of wealth, happiness, and abundance in my life that I am immensely grateful for every day.

I have found writing the ending to this book harder than I thought it would be. As a coach, I tend to have an ongoing relationship with my clients, so I get to hear how they are getting on. I would love to hear about your progress, so please reach out and connect with me. Tell me what you thought of this book and let me know how you are getting on with the tools and techniques. You can find me on Facebook under my name or you can email me via the website www.jorichings.com

Please share this book with anyone you know who is either going through difficult times right now or who has been through tough times (which is probably just about everyone you know!)

Much love and bucketful's of gratitude,

Jo Richings

xx

ABOUT THE AUTHOR

Jo Richings still lives in South Bristol, UK.

Along with her daughter Abby, she has also co-written two books for children which explain some of the concepts in this book:

Oscar meets his Worry Chimp

How to Stop Worrying

Both are available on Amazon as paperback or Kindle